Letting Go of Heaven

Laura Steffens & Adina M. Kring

WESTBOW
PRESS®
A DIVISION OF THOMAS NELSON
& ZONDERVAN

WestBow Press books may be ordered through booksellers or by contacting:

WestBow Press
A Division of Thomas Nelson & Zondervan
1663 Liberty Drive
Bloomington, IN 47403
www.westbowpress.com
1 (866) 928-1240

ISBN: 978-1-5127-9930-9 (sc)
ISBN: 978-1-5127-9931-6 (hc)
ISBN: 978-1-5127-9929-3 (e)

Library of Congress Control Number: 2017912945

Print information available on the last page.

WestBow Press rev. date: 03/22/2019

Dedication

I dedicate this book to my husband Trevor,
who never let go of my hand,
to my daughter Claire, who taught me how to love,
and to the Grace to the Nations' family, who prayed me through.
                                                    Adina Kring

Contents

Chapter Nine

Chapter Ten

Chapter Eleven

Acknowledgement

As there are far too many wonderful people to thank, we will not try to name them all individually to ensure we forget no one. But we do want every one of you who contributed to the creation of this book to know how much you are appreciated, valued and loved. We thank you for all your sacrifice and service. May the Lord always richly bless you!

Foreword by Reverend LaNora Morin

My husband, Jody and I pulled up to our friend's house on Sunday afternoon, February 5th, 2012, to watch the Super Bowl. A lot of our church family were getting together to watch the game and celebrate our friend's daughter's birthday. At that moment, I received a phone call from my friend, Rae O, Pastor of Grace to the Nations in Tucson, Arizona. She was calling to let me know that Adina, one of my precious spiritual daughters, was lingering between life and death. Hearing Pastor Rae's frightened and tearful voice describe what had happened to Adina, caused my heart to sink as I realized we may not have Adina even through the end of that very day if God did not do a miracle! Jody and I sat in the car and prayed and then went into the party to let our church family know. Most everyone there knew Adina. She and Trevor, her husband, would come to visit us at Fountain of Life at various times for special events. Prayer for Adina started at that Super Bowl party and continued around the clock at our church for several days. Like so many who were impacted by this event, I had to make a conscious choice to position myself in faith and lay aside the "what ifs" with their accompanying fears.

The following day, my daughter, Melanie, and I drove to Tucson to pray for Adina and encourage Trevor and our friends at Grace. When we walked into the hospital, we were stunned to see the crowd of faithful friends and family all holding prayer vigil outside the

ICU. Immediately, Pastor Rae and Trevor came to us and gave us the latest update. The prognosis was grim. Yet, I saw such determination in both of them as the others gathered round. Trevor took us into Adina's room and gave us a few minutes with her. The sight of my spiritual daughter who is so vivacious and bubbly lying there so lifeless was almost more than I could stand. Something inside of me was stronger than the emotions I felt. The Holy Spirit gave me a glimpse into the truth...not the facts...and my spirit began to agree with His Word. I can't remember what I spoke to Adina, but I do remember I reminded her of His Word and His plans for her life. Melanie took Adina by the hand and said "You're not done here. There's much more you are supposed to accomplish. I know you don't want to come back, but you must!"

One of the most remarkable things I witnessed was the depth of God that flowed from Trevor's heart. Trevor was like a gallant warrior with fire and fight in his eyes one minute and a gracious, compassionate host the next. He fought for Adina's life with resolve and courage when he prayed and interceded. Then, he would bring calm and confidence to the friends and family when he would announce to them her latest status. I told him God had clearly anointed him to walk through this valley of the shadow of death without wavering. He had an assurance that only heaven can give to someone who knows Jesus.

Besides reading the inspirational and intriguing story shared here of Adina's miraculous experience in Heaven and her recovery to normal life, you will be challenged in your own walk with God. The true test of our faith in God and the work of His Word in our lives comes during the fiery furnace of affliction. As you read, my prayer is that your life will be changed, not just inspired. Life brings to us many good things. However, there are also times we go through that can cause us to become bitter and angry, or mold us more and more into His character and nature. This is what I have seen happen in Trevor and Adina. Their walk with God is so much sweeter and so much deeper than before this happened. As well, they have His compassion that longs for all to be saved and for none to perish. How does one prepare for such times as what this couple walked through? The times when unexpected, unwanted, world-rocking kind of events threatens to destroy our lives are the times when we will be dependent on what we have stored up in our hearts of God and His Word. This is when we must know Him!

May this book stir your hunger to know Jesus more and to increase your faith to believe for the impossible!

For His Glory,

Pastor LaNora Morin
April 14, 2016

Preface by Trevor Kring

This book is the result of one of the most difficult and trying times in the life of Adina and me. In fact, her life almost ended several times. The events described on the following pages will lead you through our journey in all of its horror, tears, pain, joy, miracles, and glory. God has truly shown He is faithful to us. He has also revealed aspects of His character and desire for His people as we went through this valley of the shadow of death in some very surprising, sometimes painful, but always life-giving ways.

It is our intention and prayer that God will reveal Himself to you and through your life as a result of reading this book. The Holy Spirit is our counselor and the One who leads us into all truth, and we pray that He will speak to you as you read. Our journey through the unknown has revealed God to us in very powerful ways and we pray reading about it will do the same for you. May you know the Father, through the Son, by the power of the Holy Spirit, in Jesus' name!

Prologue by Laura Steffens

A couple days following Adina's hospital release, I walked into her living room where she sat with a friend recouping. Like everyone else, I wanted to hear about my friend's experience. I wondered-**no hoped**-she would share her heavenly impressions. Did she see angels, the throne, or did she meet Jesus face to face? Pavlov's dog had nothing on me while anticipating her description of the miraculous.

Interrupting them watching a video, the DVD player was stopped on a close-up of a blank page entitled, "Chapter 1." I incorrectly assumed they were watching a tutorial on how to write a book. As a writer and professional journalist always looking for interesting topics needing development, I was eager to take a leap of faith and instantly committed to help my friend write what assuredly would be a most amazing story.

It seemed nearly everyone asked Adina to write a book detailing her experience. What I did not know was earlier the same day she prayerfully asked the Lord, "Do you want me to tell people about this?" He said, "Yes, I want you to write a book." She thought in her heart, "I'm not a writer. This can't be God." So she put a fleece before Him and knew if this was the Lord, He would confirm. She said, "If my friend Laura Steffens offers to help me write my story, I will accept that as a sign from you Lord, and I will do it."

Previous to Adina's crisis, I made vacation plans so was not in Tucson during the greater portion of her hospital stay. Perhaps that was by divine intervention. But in little more than a month from the date of the incident, we began drafting her vision before memories had a chance to be altered or influenced. Although often discombobulated, Adina's friends drove her weekly to my home, as she was not able to function wholly on her own. So began the journey of writing her story. She walked tenaciously, seeming fearful at times, clearly transmuted by her obvious hardship.

At the start, much of our meeting time was spent in tears. We would begin each session with prayer, and in the beginning often got little else done in between bouts of crying or anguished moments. The phantasmagoria in her mind played across her face and gave her eyes a sort of haunting appearance. I knew my friend was struggling and was not sure how best to comfort her. But we talked. She would share, we prayed, and I asked questions, sometimes for hours at a time.

I am so glad to have been there in some small way to help my friend, if only to hold her hand as she cried. I guess she wept for herself, but her grief was due in great part to the loss of closeness she felt in God's presence. Beside herself with sorrow, she grieved over lost treasure. As she notes in the chapter on heaven, so many things happened that were too marvelous for words and our attempt here to convey what she experienced is earthly at best.

Advised to tell the story in her own words, Adina realized she could benefit from professional help. The faithfulness of my friend to our commitment and her faith in my ability as a writer is touching. Even though I tried my best to write in compliment to Adina's voice, our composition journey was not about personal pursuits. Those who know Adina might say the essence of the book does not sound like her voice. But Adina is a chameleon. With some friends she speaks street smart. With the more traditional or formally educated, she talks with a vocabulary that befits her audience, and with Christians, as a student of the Word; she knows how to speak *Christianese*. She is ready in or out of season *(2 Timothy 4:2)*, with a voice all her own that has become as scripture says "…all things to all men..." *(1 Corinthians 9:22-23)*. During discussions Adina declared, "This book is not about 'my voice,' but rather about reflecting God's voice. Our effort is not so my voice can be heard, but rather about God's message being shared. This is His-story!"

So listen for the Lord's voice, legible in every line.[i] I assure you, Adina's voice is on every page too. And as you learn the details of her ordeal, maybe you will hear my voice on occasion along with a slew of doctors, friends and family. Readers should note while Adina tells her story, there are also many other people speaking throughout the book. Often they are quoted and when this occurs, quotation marks are placed around their comments. But if someone speaks at length, you will find their monologue in an indented paragraph of text proceeded by reference to the speaker to guide you through the many contributors to this work. As well, many medical terms or faith-based concepts are introduced and discussed in the book. Please review the glossary of terms for meaning or greater understanding. But most importantly, listen for the Lord's inspirational message: His Word and purpose, His promise, salvation and mostly His great love[ii] (the real gem of this book). We prayerfully hope God is made real and tangible as you read, beginning now and forevermore.

Be blessed in Him.

CHAPTER ONE

In The Beginning

"How do you know me?...I saw you
sitting under the tree...."
John 1:48 (paraphrased)

I remember seeing crimson leaves, an earmark of autumn in up-state New York, symbolizing yet another seasonal mix of rich and creamy yellow vegetation---not unlike sunset, burnt brown and rustic orange foliage all declaring the beauty of fall. I ran outside. It could have been a thousand things causing the desire to escape. I needed to break out of my cage. But I felt alone and isolated so I ran to seek solace from my tree. I walked to the sidewalk paralleling our front porch and stopped. Looking up I saw my old friend a majestic oak tree that stood in the front of our two-story home. The tree's majesty far surpassed the appearance of the cookie-cutter house we lived in, but if not for the sunlight coming through the branches this would not have been a miraculous moment. My tree was breathtaking. "The light," a new—brighter source—its own light, was dancing in between the leaves. What was it I wondered, a squirrel, a bird, or was it an enormous insect? In my eleven year old mind, I wondered how light flickered through the trees like a butterfly, fluttering high and then low. I remember a peace fell over me as I stood in awe of this idyllic scene.

"Is that you God?" I asked in a soft and quiet whisper.

I watched the light until it disappeared, taking at least two minutes as the radiant sparkle ignited then sputtered and faded. I felt the world come rushing towards me, screeching to a halt, then the moment passed and I returned to my adolescent reality. Turmoil describes my childhood home, of which the details are different depending on to whom you talk. Suffice to say, we were definitely not the ideal family, nor did we represent a model of tranquil home life.

Odd I thought of heavenly things in a moment like that, because I definitely believed there was no God. My mom wanted me, my brother and two sisters to be in church, but my parents did not regularly attend. In principal they thought it was pivotal for us to be there, but it was not important enough to put Christian-living into practice in our daily lives. The juxtaposition of wanting to believe in God and the evidence, in my life anyway, that He did not exist was the cause of many confusing and contradictory moments as I sought to know Him. Every autumn passed, one after another, and during each I asked many eternally-focused questions, the answers to which are now a greater reality in my life because of my own near death experience.

Prior to the February 2012 incident, my childhood experiences and memories, both good and bad, framed my character to become a brazen, combative, confident and self-reliant woman, an extreme thrill-seeker who needed to be at the center of attention at any party, event or crowd. Certainly I was not a candidate to join the convent, the Peace Corps, or the Neighborhood Watch.

I was always reaching out to people though, everybody's friend, still I was hard to get to know, much less understand. My many friendships truly embody the concept of six degrees of separation from Kevin Bacon.[1] But even close acquaintances only knew a part of me, only saw one or two aspects of what formed my broader personality. Few shared my life outside the world they knew me in. Malibu Barbie's and Hell's Angels do not normally hang, if you know what I mean. Yet my friends encompassed all walks of life, all peoples, all ages, shapes, colors and sizes. I had a revelation about the colorful tapestry that exemplifies my network and their connections.....they are all different, but they all have the same kind of heart. I *love* because I see their heart.

How does someone go from being my own form of atheistic doubter to questioning a miraculous moment in time? As a child I spoke directly to the Lord with such sincerity while at the same time disbelieving He even heard my prayers; or worse, He heard them but did not care. Learning what faith meant was a journey that took me and my family nearly thirty years and thirty days[2] since my visit to the oak tree. But the upheaval was worth the effort. The events which brought me ***revelation*** are most likely not unlike events in your own life, questions you have asked, or doubts you may have had. But I would not suggest taking the same horrific detour I did to find my revelation or my God! That is why I share my story hoping you will be inspired and desire to live with a more heavenly mind set, while learning to speak to God directly and expecting Him to answer.

---

[1] "Six degrees of separation:" is a popular theory fostering the idea everyone is only six steps away from anyone else on the planet. Through introduction everyone can be connected via a friend through a maximum of six others.

[2] Roughly the time between standing outside my house looking at the oak tree, until February 5th, 2012, the date of the incident.

Dear Reader,

I bless you and pray as you read my story you too would find your own path. I believe you are either already a believer or are genuinely seeking to know Him better. Therefore, I also believe God will uniquely reveal Himself to you as He has to me. I pray He wakens you to His great love and that you would know Him as intimately as I have come to know Him. It is His will that none should perish *(2 Peter 3:9)*. He sets before you blessings and curses, life and death. Choose life[3] my friends, I have!

His alone,

Adina M. Kring

---

[3] Deuteronomy 30:19

CHAPTER TWO

The Incident

For there is hope for a tree, if it be cut down,
that it will sprout again, and that
its shoots will not cease.
Job 14:7 (NKJV)

Sundays at Grace to the Nations (GTTN),[4] the multi-cultural, multi-generational church I attended in Tucson, Arizona, were always chaotic, especially when we had a guest speaker. You know, like your mother-in-law coming to visit, everything must be clean. Do you have extra toilet paper in the bathrooms? What is happening with Pastor Rae's microphone and are there refreshments in the Green Room? Basically, I always took it upon myself to make sure all the details of church function were in order and the way I knew my pastor would want them to be.

February 5th, 2012, started out basically like any other Sunday! Guest speaker Robby Booth, who had just finished a marriage conference the day before, had come to address both congregations (English and Spanish services). He was in the Green Room with his wife Bonita, Pastor Rae Orozco, her seven-year old daughter Gigi,

---

[4] Grace to the Nations is abbreviated "GTTN," or is referred to as "Grace."

and me. We were joking, laughing and having a great time sharing travel stories about the ministry. You know those anecdotes where people are eating monkey brains....no honestly; this is not just a scene from *Indiana Jones and the Temple of Doom*. It was real! I ate monkey brains while on a mission's trip to India. I guess in a country where they worship cows, creative alternatives to beef are inevitable. Basically I was told we sat around exchanging food horror stories. I say "I am told" because the week prior to the incident is gone from my mind. Essentially for me every moment, conversation and event never happened. I have no memory of the incident or the particulars leading up to my lost consciousness. So if you owe me money, now would be the time to step up. "I'm just saying." Please know as you read on, many of those who witnessed the episode have filled in the blanks for me.

One of the joys of ministry is sharing your lives and all the humor different situations can present when dealing with people and God's work. Meeting Robby and his wife Bonita was such a pleasure and one of those rare moments when we were able to relax and put our feet up. Pastor Rae was relating how she and I enjoy adventures together because we can talk and chuckle at life and serving people. We have on occasion even been accused of being drunk, while strapped into airliner seats, because we were giggling out of control on one of our many ministry flights.

During my first mission's trip I was baptized, as they say in Christian circles, in the most extreme way by taking a trip (an adventure really) to a Native American reservation touring in a small Cessna, and again on another trip to India. We roared with laughter, recounting my terror as I shared how I learned "I am a white knuckle flyer." You know the type of passenger who digs their nails into the arm chair of their seat while holding their breath in absolute horror. I am afraid of heights and was flying in a tiny two-seater passenger plane, literally with a hole in the middle of the floor boards. No kidding! I could see the ground intermittently with the cloudy atmosphere passing under my feet. I was thinking, "We're gonna' die!" But I did not want Pastor Rae to know about my fear because she would not allow me to go with her on trips. The whole flight I did not move and kept praying under my breath declaring to the Lord, "I know your thoughts towards me…I know I'm not gonna' die…I know the plans you have for me…and they don't include my dead body on the ground below." I was trying to talk myself down. "Yah, I have a future," I hoped! We laughed until we cried. We bonded while sharing *work of the gospel* war stories.

911 Call

Robby Booth had just finished his first service message, a continuation of the conference-theme, and a hilarious monologue on marital relations. He was heading into the Latino service for a repeat performance when things took an unusual turn. I began to experience an itchy sensation in my throat. Along with swelling of the tongue and an ever growing *dyspneic* shortness of breath, I was going into a heightened state of anaphylaxis, otherwise known as a sudden and severe allergic reaction. Having eaten a pineapple chunk from a container of assorted fruit which I set out earlier for our Green Room guests, the all too familiar sensation caught me by surprise. Previously, I had never demonstrated an allergy to pineapple. The Booths noticed I was reacting oddly too. Due to a history of food allergies, I told Pastor Rae, *I was feeling funny.* She gave me two *Benadryl* and we waited for the symptoms to subside.

Five minutes later, I was standing with my hand gripping the counter. Bonita asked, "What's wrong?" She instructed me to sit down and began to pray for me. Lying down, standing-up, or leaning, none of it was working. I could not breathe. Pastor Rae also noted I was acting peculiar. She is always so in tune with my moods, always checking in. She is so aware.

"Are your lips swelling?" she asked.

"Pastor I feel weird," I said while struggling to catch my breath. "I'm having a hard time swallowing," as I sat down clutching hand to throat.

"Call *9-1-1!*" I choked out in a raspy voice.

So Robby made the initial call, while I continued trying to clear my throat. A female operator began to ask pertinent questions, so Pastor Rae took the phone as Robby was needed in the sanctuary.

"Is she allergic?"

"She's having an anaphylactic reaction. Yah, I think she ate something she's allergic to," declared Rae. "I am familiar with anaphylaxis. I had it myself and I'm gonna' hit her with the Epi[5]."

"Please don't do that. It could harm her," said the operator. Then she asked, "Is it her prescription?"

"No, it's mine," said Rae.

"Please wait for the EMTs. They're on their way. Don't do it," asserted the operator.

"Okay, I'm not going to but only because you said so," emphasized Rae reluctantly.

The operator was not there to see my extreme condition and made a bad call. Rae had me lie down while I prayed. My situation grew worse going from bad to dangerous in mere seconds. "Jesus help me!" were the last words I spoke before actively choking. My

---

[5] Epi is a slang term for EpiPen.

airway was restricted preventing oxygen from reaching the lungs. In response to the blockage, my throat began to swell and I entered an acute allergic reaction stage where medical professionals say, *death is imminent.* The operator insisted Rae stay on the line until they arrived. It took seven minutes for the EMTs to get there. Rae speaking for herself:

> Adina was looking at me with a lot of fear and bewilderment; well more shock than actual fear. I kept telling her, "Look at me. You're going to be okay. You're going to be okay." Which I never doubted, I really never did, with one exception. At the hospital I went through a moment of uncertainty. I stepped outside the ER and spoke out loud, "Lord, Lord, I can't lose her," Otherwise, I was confident He would not allow any real harm to come to my dear friend.

By the time the EMTs arrived, I was starting to convulse. Thrashing on the chaise, I struggled for breath anticipating rescue efforts. He could not get the tracheal intubation tube down my throat to facilitate ventilation. My lung pathway was completely blocked. While the EMTs placed me in restraints, not unlike a seatbelt, they strapped me onto the stretcher. I was fully convulsing. Gigi, Pastor Rae's daughter, saw this and asked, "Why is Adina flopping like a fish?"

Seeing rapidly twitching muscles from repeated contraction and expansion was too much for a seven year old, and she began to cry. Rae clutched her baby knowing how disturbing it was for one so young to see someone considered a close friend in distress. (I am like a surrogate mother to Gigi. We have a precious bond; a "BFF" friendship). "I left Gigi with a friend. I needed to be with Trevor," said Pastor Rae.

She made the decision to join my husband Trevor Kring who had arrived on the scene, so she released guardianship, put on her pastor's hat and went to do the job she is well-equipped to do. Her plan was to pray for me and to support Trevor. EMTs wheeled me into their vehicle, closed the ambulance doors and prepared to drive the *1.5* miles to the hospital, which took roughly three minutes.

Prior to my allergy attack, Trevor went to grab us a taco lunch and had only been gone about fifteen minutes. He pulled into the church parking lot and was turning the key in the ignition when he saw the red fire department rescue transport. At about the same time, he received a call from our friend Johnnie F.

> "Hey man. It's Johnnie," he said.
>
> "What's with the ambulance?" Trevor asked.
>
> "It's your wife."
>
> "If you're kidding, it's not funny. What's going on?"
>
> "I'm not kidding. It's Adina," Johnnie said. "Where are you?"
>
> "I'm in the parking lot," Trevor said with concern. "I'm on my way."

Johnnie is a close friend of ours and someone with whom we always jest. We tease because I often make prophetic commentary when we call him "Reverend Johnnie F." Trevor knew he was serious at the mention of my name. I bet he freaked. During our relationship history, one visit to the urgent care facility for a breathing treatment was the extent of medical crises. Never before had he seen anything on this scale. Trevor ran across the church's soccer field, part of him trying to run faster, while the other half was reluctant, not knowing how to respond. He was in shock! He questioned should he hold back, run up to the ambulance, or stop and wait for directions. The ambulance doors slammed shut. Lost in the moment, he heard Pastor Rae calling him from the facility breezeway.

> "Trevor, there you are. I've been looking for you. It's Adina, we gotta' go," said Rae with an authoritative tone.

> "Johnnie is in the parking lot," Trevor said.

> "I'll meet you there," she replied.

The Emergency Room

Before the ambulance drove off, Johnnie pulled up behind and parked. He saw me awake and sitting up with an oxygen mask clasped to my mouth. He was preparing to trail behind the emergency vehicle when Rae asked to ride along. The ambulance already in motion, Rae, Trevor and Gigi piled in his four-door sedan. Rae began to pray, while Trevor buckled-in Gigi. Following immediately behind the ambulance, sirens blared as traffic parted. The ambulance stopped at the ER entrance and Pastor Rae handed my purse to Trevor who followed the stretcher inside. After parking the car, Johnnie and Rae went to the public waiting room.

> "Who are you?" questioned one staff member trying to manage the disorder and clear the area.

> "I'm her husband Trevor Kring." Following directions, he stood near the emergency room[6] entry way where a computer was located for gathering insurance information.

---

[6] The Emergency Room is often referred to as the ER throughout this book.

One of the hospital staff offered periodic updates saying, "We lost her in the ambulance once and we lost her in the emergency room. She is not breathing on her own." Report during the ambulance ride was *I coded* and my airway was completely restricted, so my heart and lungs stopped. Varying reports claimed my brain was starved of oxygen for anywhere from seven to twelve minutes.[7] Concerns included whether or not I would regain consciousness, or had sustained significant damage. Medical sources report without oxygen, permanent brain damage can begin as early as **four minutes**, and death can occur as soon as **eight**. EMT's moved me into the ER bay, where my husband met with medical personnel.

A hospital physician assigned to the task of keeping family informed stated, "...emergency room staff tried to *trach her.*" She was very gracious in keeping everyone up to date and opened a private room reserved for difficult cases. This allowed family to pray privately and be together without interference. Trevor noted it was an intensely emotional time as she escorted them to the room, even praying on occasion while intermittently checking on them. "I went out three or four times to be with Gigi and to check on her," Rae said. Gigi asked, "Is she going to be okay?" Rae replied, "She is going to be okay Honey, but let's keep praying." *Anaphylaxis* is a serious allergic reaction known for a rapid onset of symptoms which can cause death in reportedly five percent of the cases (roughly one out of every twenty incidents).[8] "The horror on the face of my young child was extreme and her reaction physical," Rae said. "It was obvious she needed to be with me. So I stayed and held her."

---

[7] Doctors did not agree on the exact amount of oxygen deprivation. Seven to sixteen minutes seems to be the range. Several doctors noted various times and could not agree on *anoxia* time frame. Notably, medical records do not agree either.

[8] Typically, such reactions result in a number of symptoms including an itchy rash, throat swelling, and low blood pressure. Common causes include insect bites or stings, food allergies, and reactions to medications.

Rae was caught amid various roles: being the pastor caring for her sheep (taking care of Trevor and all the Grace members who came to support me), and being my close friend and counselor. Also, being able to function as mother to help her littlest one process what might have been one of the most frightening and dreadful events of her young life was just one more thing to juggle. Besides the fact she is a woman (all women, by nature, multitask), how does anyone keep that kind of composure? Rae called her husband, Pastor Obed Orozco, who had just finished translating second service for Robby. He had no idea what transpired when service started, but he needed to remove Gigi from the trauma.

> "Obed, I'm losing Adina. It's not looking good," wept Rae. Pastor came immediately to the hospital to support everyone. He rushed over, met with Trevor for a second, and took Gigi home.

> "I stayed there until 2:30 p.m., in the private waiting room," said Rae. "General internist, Dr. Fredy T informed us she had just been wheeled to ICU."

> Dr. Fredy[9] sat with Trevor and Pastor Rae a moment, then blurted out, "What…happened to her?"

> At that moment, Trevor was hit by the ominous nature of it all.

> "How did she get here?" Dr. Fredy asked again.

The situation seemed surreal. It would be several hours into

---

[9] **Please note:** For the sake of this story, Dr. Fredy T was not personally interviewed. All quotes come from conversations he had with others and are based on their recollection of the conversation(s), and do not reflect Dr. T's personal words, dialogue or thoughts.

surgery when Dr. Fredy returned to speak with Trevor and Rae. He wanted clarification as to what actually occurred prior to hospital arrival. At this time they believed my asthma was dangerously out of control, and had been for the past few weeks. The pineapple allergy had yet to be diagnosed, and doctors could not say with confidence an allergic reaction was the cause of the medical drama. He explained my airway was gradually getting tighter. Because my body's reaction was progressive and subtle, he claimed I would not have noticed a decline in thoracic cavity function. All it took was one big event and my airway closed completely causing my lungs and heart to stop.

As a side bar, I have heard it said allergies are cumulative. What that means is for those who have allergic tendencies (which I do-- asthma and all), we can eat something every day and never have a problem. The night before, Trevor brought home a fresh pineapple which we devoured. In the morning, just eating one piece set-off a chain reaction. Once the body reaches the saturation point, drastic medical steps are required to restore health. We were unaware I was allergic to pineapple, but eating it triggered a severe asthma attack. Pastor was shocked by how quickly the situation went from laughter to alarm. One moment the day was pretty much like any Sunday ministering to the body of believers, and next I was fighting for my life. The doctor's boldness was impressive. He spoke bluntly without trying to sugar-coat hospital events. He laid it out and summed it up.

> "Listen, here's what's happening," Dr. Fredy, spoke in a firm but knowledgeable voice. "It is very grim. I don't know if she will make it through the night. Swelling of the brain causes problems. We'll put everything to sleep, but when we have to bring her out, it can be really bad. So, I'm not going to give you a lot of hope. We will see what happens!"

Pastor Rae extended her hand touching Trevor's arm. Speaking softly under her breath saying, "Steady."

"Can I see her?" asked Trevor.

"Of course you can." The doctor warned, "but be prepared. She has a lot of tubes, is sedated, and has been put into a drug induced paralysis."

Trevor hoisted himself up and gingerly moved toward the door where he paused a moment. He went alone, needing time by himself. Gearing up, he entered the emergency treatment unit where I laid with my eyes rolled back in my head. Secured by every monitor and machine hooked-up to dispense life, equipment designed to safely deliver a steady flow of oxygen to my lungs, I appeared lifeless. He returned to the waiting room a few minutes later visibly shaken. Then Pastor Rae came into the room. She was angry!

I was mad at the devil. How dare he seize Adina's life and try to take her like that? The devil could not reach his claws in and take what was dedicated to the Lord. From that moment on, I was livid. That's where I got my strength for the rest of the people. This was a demonic attack, and not part of the natural course of life. I knew this just wasn't the way she was going to die. I became defiant, and the power and authority of the Word came over me. I spoke prophetically over my friend, "You will live and not die... *(Psalms 118:17)*...for I know that my Redeemer lives and **you** shall stand on the earth in the latter day...In [your] flesh [you] shall see God" *(Job 19:25-26)*. "She's going to live. She won't die."

15

It was a bold statement. Sometimes faith is defiance and defiance is faith.

Trevor agreed and declared, "No, she won't die!"

Rae and Trevor were together agreeing for miracles from heaven, while gathering their thoughts and building up their faith. "We're gonna' go to war!" Rae professed. Asserting even more, she added:

> Trevor constantly spoke the *Word of the Lord*, exhorting others to believe God could do the impossible. Often on the verge of exhaustion, he insisted our faith stay strong on behalf of Adina. His trust was the weapon God used to keep him strong and focused. Trevor was a champ! I have seen much older, stronger men wither under this kind of assault, but he did not fail to be her guardian or to defend her cause before the Lord. Although he wept while working through disbelief and bewilderment, he was always hopeful and never gave into despair. His level of faith never changed and his belief God was going to walk her through the crisis never wavered. "We are going to plan right now as though you may have to wheel her around for a while, but we are going to live like she is going to walk out of this [hospital] on her own two feet."

This kind of faith and support did not extend just to Trevor, but spread to others. Pastor, grieving in her own way and for her own reasons, knew she had to be strong for both family and church.

> When I saw all the babies in Christ [new believers] sitting in the waiting room, I knew what this attack was all about, and I spoke aloud, "I see what the foul

demon who attacked Adina is trying do. He wants
to give God a bad name and to frighten newcomers."

I was known, among other titles, as the Connections Pastor,
someone commissioned as a bridge to the community and overseer of
all new members, visitors and guests who attended our congregation.
I contacted people coming into the church to determine how we
could help meet their needs and assist them in finding ways to
connect to the Lord and the things of God, including linking them
with other church family. No doubt, it was many of my friends and
so many of my older friends (both secular and Christian) who came
to see me at the hospital. All I know is people came to sit and wait
for me to recover. Some cried, some worried, but everyone prayed.

No Walls

Overwhelming hope can be summarized in a vision seen by Pastor
Obed. He often has prophetic dreams, which occasionally reveal
walls around people who are going to die.

"Obed, I refuse to lose her," declared Rae.

Later that night he said, "I don't see any walls Rae."

This statement was crucial and his vision meant a lot, reinforcing
Rae's commitment to stand strong against the plaguing fears and
doubts. After the ambulance madness and induction into hospital
melee (the opposite of church protocol), *waiting* became the new
agenda.

CHAPTER THREE

The Waiting Game

...there is a friend that sticks closer than a brother.
Proverbs 18:24 (ESV)

Having friends is so previous to me, but ***girlfriends***, sister-soldiers will take you to a whole "...'nother level."[10] I do not know how any woman survives without them. Women are compassionate, possessing strong hearts, like love incubators, and are natural nurturers. I feel sorry for those who have never felt the care of a sister. Having girlfriends is so important, and at no time was this more real in my life.

One of the most miraculous things about this ordeal were the tearful moments when I learned about dear friends, like Joni G, Jacque R, Katrina O, and Pastor Carol who stayed with me throughout my hospital days. Joni and many more were by my side in prayer and support during thirteen days of trouble. Even the staff could not believe the influx of visitors. Joni G stayed in ICU and later in recovery. Every day she held my hand, comforting and consoling. Remarkably, she was with me from day two and did

---

[10] Street slang: referencing "whole other level."

not quit her daily vigil until I was released on February 17th. Joni explains how she first learned of my situation.

> Adina and I usually hung out every Monday. It was a time for prayer and to focus on rebuilding a foundation of trust, to renew our spirits and our friendship. So as always, I texted:
>
> "G-o-o-d –m-o-r-n-i-n-g!"
>
> Twenty minutes later, I texted again.
>
> "W-h-a-t—a-r-e—w-e—d-o-i-n-g—t-o-d-a-y?"
>
> Five minutes later the phone rang,
>
> "Hi!"
>
> I heard Trevor's voice.
>
> "Are you sitting down?"
>
> A little annoyed, I responded, "Why?"
>
> It did not dawn on me something dreadful happened. Then he asked if I was driving. Now slightly irritated, I told him I was home and asked him to explain.
>
> "What's going on?"
>
> He said Adina was in ICU and had gone into anaphylactic shock. I asked where they were keeping her and left my house in my pajamas (a

uniform really: black pants and a black shirt) and drove directly to the hospital.

Trevor met Joni in the waiting room and walked her back to ICU. She remembered seeing others, but said their faces were a blur. "I just wanted to see Adina. I had my Bible, and I was going to pray over her. I was ready for war," Joni said.

It was also a god-thing when Joni came back into my life. We had a falling out that lasted for two and a half years and had just reconciled our twenty-year relationship. It was weird, knowing I had a sister, well a friend as close as one, and that we were not talking. Still I was always concerned for her, asked about and prayed for her. I love her! I believe our calamity was caused by personal misunderstandings and because I was so naive, not realizing how things can happen when you are in ministry. I was not prepared for attacks that the Bible tells us will come (*2 Timothy 3:12*). In short, our relationship was hindered. I knew God had to restore our hearts. Two months before the incident, Joni showed up at midnight and we talked until dawn.

"I knew she wouldn't turn me away regardless. I needed a friend, my friend, my family," Joni said.

Commenting about herself, Joni says she is "much better in a crisis than in real life." But she is so precious to me. I understand what she meant by her statement. Some of us come from a dark past where we had to learn to survive. In spite of the dark, we see reality very well…it is a gift we offer to others struggling to find their way. We develop a sort of night vision. Joni demonstrated this same kind of passion, care and concern on my behalf. This event has knit us together, this time forever.

Intensive Care Unit

On heavy life support, Joni, moved with compassion, rubbed my feet because they were cold, and my hands she smothered in lotion. She also read the Bible, psalm after psalm. She spoke, reading aloud from God's word, His truth, the blessings and promises laced throughout scripture.

I have often told all my friends and husband too, if anything were ever to happen to me, get the strongest prayer warriors to stand watch and to proclaim the Word over my situation. No lie! Prior to the incident, I said this same thing to my best friend Jacque R more than once. I told her and others "Wash me with the truth of God's Word. Read to me. Sing praises over me. Do not stop ministering to my inner man using God's Word." I literally pleaded with my girlfriends. Joni was one of many unsung and unseen warriors who battled. Each day she spoke hope in the drab enclave of a hospital intensive care unit. Why I asked people to pray over me seems odd now, but strangely prophetic at the same time. Thankfully many did just that. They read to me, played music and waited on God to intervene.

> What I always feared has happened to me. What I
> dreaded has come true.
>
> *(Job 3:25, NLT)*

Others did the same in the following days. Another friend, Katrina O, a street savvy gospel gangster who was barely coming into her spiritual destiny, kept vigilant night watch. She sat by my bed and read beginning every morning at three. Friends found her asleep the next day leaning over me with her arms spread across my torso and her head resting on my chest like scripture's Rizpah who protected her sons from the birds and wild animals *(2 Samuel 21:10)*. It was not the battle-scarred prayer warriors who stayed during the desolate hours of the night, but rather the newbies, new converts, eager Christians and the little lambs, as scripture calls them, who were moved by compassion and inspired by the Holy Spirit to bless me in a way that I cannot express without tears. Thank you everyone! Later when I asked Joni to describe what happened, she said she prayed without expectation. She only hoped some sort of peace would come over me. She was convinced I could hear her, and frankly, I think I did. Joni knew if I was hearing anything, I would want it to be the Word of God.

The ICU was darkly lit, yet reminiscent of sunset, I suppose to create false comfort in the midst of clashing kingdoms. Time passed, one minute collapsing unseen into the next. The room was icy too, but alive with monitors beeping and people shuffling from one piece of machinery to another. One picture window looked outside over a big tree in a small courtyard. It seems the monumental moments in my life are often marked by the presence of resplendent trees. Christian music played softly in the background. Jacque brought in speakers and an iPod, which played seven (the number of perfection) prophetic songs in one continuous loop: *My God is More than Enough, Greater is He That is in Me, More Than Anything, Great is Your Mercy, Moving Forward, Glory,* and *Your Name.* These extremely prophetic songs that once echoed battle cries throughout my days now surrounded me as I lingered between death and life. I suspect the sound of worship and their voices kept my body attached to my spirit. Once again, I marvel at how God works in and through us in every circumstance. While in the room holding my hand, Joni watched my stats on a monitor. Light signals flashed across the screen like radar, first my heart... bleep, bleep, bleep, then blood pressure, bleep, bleep, bleep, and other stats too, bleep, bleep.

"Adina looked seriously horrific. She was unconscious. My friend Adina was just g-o-n-e," Joni exclaimed.

Emergency room staff performs life saving measures in a rush. I guess they have to when responding to the immediate needs of heart, head, bleeding or breathing, all issues requiring heroic steps to save one's life. They used white tape wrapped tightly around my head to secure the breathing tube. This visual disturbed Joni who describes her experience:

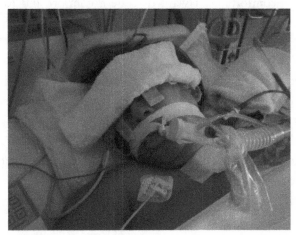

PHOTO 3-1: Headshot of Adina in the ICU Ward.

Without concern for her appearance or comfort, the medical team had quickly set up monitors, breathing machines, and various life support items that encircled her hospital bed. I saw Adina's hair was caught in the tape used to secure a respirator to her mouth. Affixed tightly to her cheeks, the tape constricted her face, which at this time was swollen above the indentation left by the adhesive. Then they put her entire body on ice packs to drop her core temperature down to 91 degrees, in an effort to help stabilize her. When I touched Adina's body, I noticed how really cold she was. Then I grabbed her hand and it was really hot. Both arms were in sleeve-like casts, legs too, and hands and feet were resting on what looked similar to heating pads. But no one had time to monitor these details. I began to rotate her hands so they would not burn and to ensure the heat was uniformly applied. I grieved because I knew Adina must have been so uncomfortable. I wanted to be a comfort and to sooth Adina, so I stroked her hair. This kind of touch, I thought, would let her know I was there.

Over twenty-eight years ago, Joni lost her mother and witnessing this spectacle with machines breathing for me, the whole episode brought her right back to that place with her own mom. Joni was miserable; a dear friend was slipping away. Inspired to pray, she got her Bible and read just like I taught her. When talking about it later, we joked how there isn't much life in life support.

Thirty minutes later, nursing staff came in to clean me up, change the bedding, reposition me, and clean away the blood and dirty linens, so Joni was asked to leave. She went to the hallway to bawl. For a few minutes she cried because having watched her mother die in this same situation, in this same hospital after three days of intensive care, just reinforced her idea that people on life support generally do not bounce back!

Later she returned to the room and held my hand until Heather T a friend and EMT, came to ICU. Heather asked if she could pray over me and grabbed my hand. I know she did not speak aloud in the physical sense, but for this baby Christian her words rang loudly in the spirit. I see now, many of the people whose lives I touched (and who have touched mine) found their **voice** for prayer. I count that as a solid victory for team Jesus. Go team!

My family had been called and told I was not expected to live. The next twenty-four hours were critical. If I survived, they were also informed I would never be the same. But Joni did not want to hear it. In Joni's mind I looked like I was actively dying. For me to return to the friend she once knew was imperative, so she prayed. Hard!

My sister Nancy was the first family member to learn about my condition. A friend of my sister, who attended Grace, called to ask about me. This phone call was the first of many guaranteeing family was notified. Immediately Nancy called my cell phone. She then called Trevor and left a message. She also called my daughter's phone. Meanwhile, Trevor returned her call.

"What's going on with my sister?" she demanded.

Trevor relayed his confusion about what happened, since they did not have definitive answers yet. Nancy clearly recalls Trevor's statement, "She is fighting for her life."

To which Nancy replied, "I'm on my way!" Nancy needed to see for herself.

Her daughters were already packing before she ended the call. Prior to leaving town, Nancy collected her thoughts by going to prayer "to get it together" before driving from Phoenix to Tucson. Emerging from her quiet place, Nancy said, "Let's hit the road." One daughter with a suitcase appeared from the bedroom and the other stepped out of the kitchen with trip provisions. "I love my kids; little troopers instantly ready for any crises," Nancy proudly stated. By the time she was in the car, prayer teams from Washington, D.C., Maryland, Virginia, and Phoenix were already engaged in intercession. "If my sister is fighting for her life, I need to be there. I would have come even if she wasn't in the fight for her life," Nancy added.

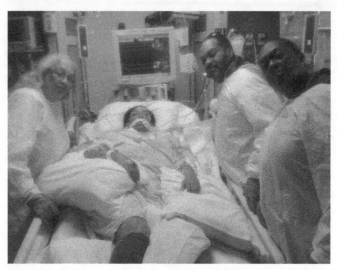

PHOTO 3-2: Family moment in ICU with an unconscious Adina. (From left to right): Mother Henrietta, brother Ricky and sister Nancy.

When the family arrived, Joni spent the rest of her time in the waiting room where she stared at the wall most days, often only setting with me for a brief 20 to 30 minute visit allowing my family to sit as only two people were allowed in the ICU at once. She described her experience like that commercial where you just sit still as life is moving in distorted hyper-motion around you, people and time rushing by in a haze, like shadows in another dimension. Besides one trip to the cafeteria to get a drink, Joni stayed in the hospital convinced if she left something might happen: I might wake up, or worse, I might never wake up. My friend stayed by my side—this kind of friendship is more than that, it is a miracle!

As for the rest of the family, most began to arrive on Monday. They took a week or so away from their busy lives to be with me, hardly leaving the intensive care unit. Basically, they were advised it was time to come and say their good-byes. Mom and brother Ricky (who live in Washington, D.C.), along with my sister Rita (who lives in Virginia), flew to Tucson. Nancy drove to the airport to meet them. My dad coming from Atlanta arrived the next day and was escorted to the hospital by a family friend.

Day two I was wheeled out for an MRI, a procedure used to diagnose extent of brain injury. It would be days before my sisters could convey incident details. My reaction was total disbelief. First of all, I had not previously been allergic to pineapple; in fact, I love it! Secondly, I am normally the person holding the hand of the one dying, praying for others and consoling the family. Basically, "I give...I minister...I don't receive ministry." It is just not standard procedure! But I am glad family, both blood relatives and spiritual, were able to be there to show solidarity and support. You have all been more than friends!

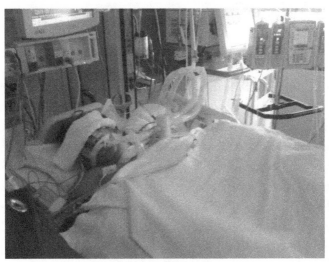

PHOTO 3-3: Adina in the ICU Ward before
waking up following surgery.

Another soul harassed by the wait was my daughter Claire. At thirteen the pandemonium she was contending with was unexpected and unimaginable. First hospital visit, she did not actually go into the room. Seeing intensive care patients clinging to technology, wearing all the accoutrements holding ailing hearts to this reality

freaked her out. The next day she tried again. Her dad dropped her
at the hospital. The family felt it was important she be there, mostly
because they know Claire is my whole world. Any hope of bringing
me through would be hastened should my baby be near.

What I learned through the hospital ordeal is waiting on God
is the answer to any life and every problem. *Psalms 46:10* tells us to,
"Be still, and know that I am God." In the waiting game, we only
find our peace in Him:

> You will keep in perfect peace those whose minds
> are steadfast, because they trust in you. Trust in the
> Lord forever, for the Lord, the Lord himself, is the
> Rock eternal.
>
> *Isaiah 26:3-4 (NIV)*

The Claire Effect

My daughter's experiences during this process were uniquely her
own. She endured a lot, but came through with flying colors. She
had been warned my affliction could result in drastic personality
changes. Naturally, she was scared I ***would be different***. Medical
staff made her wear sterile gloves in an attempt to restrict any
bacterial growth. Choking back tears, she entered the room bathed
in muted afternoon light. Throat burning, her steps cautious, she
stopped in the middle of the room just to take it all in. Trevor
encouraged her to talk to me. "Hi Mom," she said. "I love you."
There was a long pause, then "I'll see you tomorrow."

Claire is very sensitive and this was a difficult thing for her to
go through. I wish her experiencing this drama could have been
prevented. She left the room, unable to cope with feelings or the
medical spectacle. There was a third visit where she held my hand
and shared about school. Claire does not remember what she said,
but a soothing zephyr filled the air with comforting sounds, words I
do not recall, but no doubt made a difference in my recovery. It was

during the fourth visit while she spoke, one of the machines started beeping in a loud, fixed alarm alerting staff my blood pressure had elevated. Surprised by the interruption, Claire covered her ears. Eyes clinched shut and face distorted by the unruly assault, her tears sliced the air as she jumped back into a standing position.

At the sound of Claire sobbing, I tried to come up off the bed. Using both arms to push myself up, I was described as momma bear rising to protect her young. What was really creepy about this whole thing is my eyes were open and I seemed conscious, although not alert or able to focus. For sure, I have no recollection of any of this. I am going on what others have said. Coming to Claire's rescue was just instinct. Some suggested I was angry because I could not get up; others said I reacted -- trying to protect Claire.

> "Mom stop!" Claire shouted. Crying, she ran out of the room pulling aside the curtains surrounding my hospital bed. She dashed to the waiting area where Trevor spent most his days.

> "Adina - in God's time!" Nancy said, as she gently put her hand out to steady me in hopes I would regain a calmer demeanor. "Claire is okay."

> Later Nancy explained what happened. "It's not your fault. Your mom was just being who she is. It was a natural reaction for her to reach out to comfort you."

The explanation seemed to calm her. Even Trevor began to reassure Claire what happened actually helped me. The doctors were looking for any kind of reaction to outside stimuli: such as eye movement, a glance, hands twitching, and every attempt to move was construed as another reason to hope. Doctors were pleased as this was the first time I had shown any emotion. At this phase, they were convinced I had sustained *global brain damage*. Apparently during Claire's exit, she pulled back the curtain exposing me to a throng of people standing there waiting to get a glimpse. Perhaps they hoped for a chance to enter the private intensive unit, or to be near all the hoopla. Maybe it was just concerned, loving friends, praying for me. Whatever, the scene caused a great deal of commotion. Frustrated by the spectator invasion, Nancy was overwhelmed and jumped to preserve order. "I knew Adina would not want this," she said. "Get out! Everybody out. Just get out!" she yelled.

The nurses came in and cleared the room. Peace, quiet, and heavy sedation were necessary to allow my body time to heal before reintroducing me to the world. In response to all this crazy turmoil, I was crying. Tears flowed down my face collecting on the massive bandages curled around my neck. Although this might seem odd [cause it sure did to the medical staff who interpreted my tearful reaction as both peculiar and promising], it was the first demonstrated non-catatonic behavior. This incident was among several highly unusual responses witnessed during sedation. The doctors cannot confirm or deny what actually happened in regards to my unusual reaction. There is so much they do not understand about brain injuries. But one thing is certain, I was exhibiting an awful lot of incomprehensible—what they described as ***impossible***—behaviors.

Subject to the Spirit

One explanation for the ***impossible*** operating in my life could be a spiritual one. I believe when your spirit man is moving according to the **Word**, it is not subject to the body. Normally the body of the *Spirit-filled believer* is subject to the spirit.[iii] Still most of us walk around driven by our flesh and its desires. When the spirit is subject to the body, it means your flesh is in control. But when your mind is committed to Christ, His Spirit rules!

For to set the mind on the flesh is death, but
to set the mind on the Spirit is life and peace
(Romans 8:6, ESV).

The prescription given to me was meant to suppress bodily
functions, but I moved regardless of medication. I propose spiritually
I was in subjection to the **Word of God**, and it is His breath that
gives life! I am aware this statement is not necessarily tangible
theology and I am surely going to rile up some scholars on this one.
Clearly, it is not my desire to develop a new doctrine! I merely seek
to rationalize the unexplainable, while noting an obvious miraculous
connection which inspired hope in my family during one of our
darkest times.

CHAPTER FOUR

We Are Family

For this reason I bow my knees before the Father,
from whom every family in heaven
and on earth is named.
Ephesians 3:14-15(ESV)

The **Holman Bible Dictionary** describes family as the *"...basic household unit which provides a person's central relationships, nurture, support, commitment and function."* I can say, "I'm down with that!" [11]

Kring, *m*y family name, was acquired by marrying Trevor. We met at church, both hungry for the things of God. Wherever I turned he was there and when he looked to his right I was there chasing after righteous things, always serving God's people. Trevor proposed the idea of love following a weekend conference at "The Call" in Tennessee. Three years after introduction, I felt the Lord convince me to marry - an arranged marriage of sorts. Now I lovingly refer to us as the "Kringdom." When we jump in the car to go somewhere, I declare, "Let's go Kringdom." You know, "Thy Kringdom come!"

What I found so interesting about the surname *Kring*, which

---

[11] The phrase, "I'm down with that..." is street slang and means you are in agreement with what was said.

comes from a Germanic root *(meaning round or ring, complete, a family circle)*, is the truly spiritual significance of our name and the meaning it has for our life. I think it is so cool because as a couple, as a family, we are always drawing others into our circle. Another way to say it is: the name *Kring* means a circle of people and that is what my life has become since completing our household with the addition of the man to whom I have committed my heart.

Like a wedding ring's symbolism, the circle represents undying love and the continual renewal of marriage vows. Circles have long been archetypes signifying timelessness, wholeness and homecoming. A circle speaks to the return of seasons and heavenly expectation. My name, in essence, speaks to who I am as a person, a woman with heavenly hope in a solid circle of family support. So when I say our family does not stop at the front door of the Kringdom home, I am speaking spiritually about profound truths for not only my own life, but the bigger family of God, *His Church*. All believers are His family and my family too.

Personal History

Imagining a picture of a Christian family is really hinting at heavenly things. Marriages are a model of Christ and His relationship with the church *(Ephesians 5:31-32)*.^{iv} Through marriage, God has done something pretty unique and remarkable through us as a couple. Every argument, challenge and trial, every success, blessing and victory God uses as a prophetic example to teach a new truth. And my tragedy was no different. Through this ordeal I have really come to understand the meaning of the word *family*.

> God sets the solitary in families.
> *Psalms 68:6 (NKJV)*

I came to Tucson a single woman with only my brother and dad living here at the time. Eventually, all the kids found their way out here from New York. Always striving to be a family, my siblings and our mother tried to share our life in hope of developing closer relationships. But we learned the hard way: family (and past memories) can be pretty painful. With the exception of me, eventually everyone left town while I stayed to eke out an existence in the *Old Pueblo*.[12]

Circumstances being what they were I let go of my blood relatives and began to create my own new family in an environment where I could fashion a fresh self-image by being whoever or whatever I wanted. I gathered others into my clique, a crazy street family, but even that was faulty. In my own way, I had my own gang, my own family, new connections. I had new mothers, sisters, brothers, aunts and uncles. In spite of my best efforts and my rag tag peeps,[13] I had no idea what family meant or what it could be, until I found Jesus. Ultimately, church became my new family, a community of roughly two-thousand people and a vast network of connections.

"Hey, my car broke down, so call Sal."

"I need help moving, so call Bill."

"I'm short on the rent, what am I gonna' do?"

"Today, this sister and her kids don't have groceries.
Hey, let's get together and meet that need."

In my best Don Corleone[14] imitation, I can hear myself say, "Take care of my family." You [almost] don't need anything outside

---

[12] A nickname for Tucson, meaning *old city* in Spanish.

[13] "Peeps" is street slang for the word "people."

[14] Vito Andolini Corleone (aka Don Corleone) is Mario Puzo's fictional character in the novel and 1972 movie of the same name, "The Godfather," who headed a fictitious mafia family.

the family. Scripture tells us God has given those who receive Him everything we need:

> "All things are yours...." *1 Corinthians 3:21, (NKJV).*

In other words, all things pertaining to godliness are readily available to those who accept Christ's gift of salvation. We can experience provision best while in a church family. This might explain the enormous amount of people who came to see and pray for me while I was at the hospital.

Eclectic at best and anything but limited, blood family in all its colorful diversity is not so odd. But I describe *"my family"* so you understand how truly unique we are. I come from African-American stock and like to think of myself as a Nubian princess. My daughter Claire, from a previous relationship, is half Jewish-American princess and half Nubian, or as I like to say, a Black-Jewish-American princess. I must admit my daughter is so beautiful with sparkly brown eyes, perfect white teeth, and soft brown hair with natural blonde highlights. She is the best kid ever, speaks, reads and writes Hebrew. She is a straight "A" student who is so kind and such a good friend. Claire is a leader among her peers and I have no doubt will become a world changer. She is strong, intelligent, funny and a little spicy just like her momma. In contrast, Trevor is a handsome white man, with fair skin, hazel eyes, and just kissing six feet tall. But most importantly, he loves and fears the Lord. Possessing this combination of qualities is not common to many men or women, for that matter. Although there is no other white person in my paternal family, my mother could pass for white. In the sixties, she modeled for stores like Macy's in Washington, D.C.. In my black family, we are called "rainbow," meaning every shade of black from white chocolate all the way down to dark.

PHOTO 4-1: Family time. (From left to right): Devon,
Henrietta, Claire, Jordan, Rita, and Ricky.

As for my church family, there are not only black people, but
every color besides. At Tucson, Arizona's GTTN there are many
different peoples. As already noted, they call themselves a multi-
generational and multi-cultured church with every type of Latino
(from Mexican, Dominican, Puerto Rican, Spanish, Brazilian,
Cuban, Peruvian), and the numbers include Nigerians, Liberians,
Asians, Native Americans, Chinese, Koreans, and white, of course.
So when doctors, nurses or other observers were perplexed at the
myriad of colorful faces and different races coming to see me, all
declaring they were my sister or my brother, my mother or my friend,
in light of this information it is easy to understand their confusion.

> Jesus replied, "Who is my mother? Who are my
> brothers?" Then he looked at those around him
> and said, "Look, these are my mother and brothers.
> Anyone who does God's will is my brother and
> sister and mother" *Mark 3:33-35, (NLT)*.

Parenting Peril

My family tree is rooted in my father Sam and mother Henrietta. She describes me as part of what she called "a difficult mothering experience." It was not until I became a mother myself that I understood how challenging the task of motherhood can be. There is no blueprint or manual with instructions. You have a baby and "good luck with that." Hospital personnel propel you out the swinging double doors of delivery and you are on your own. Being a mom is not an easy job and the more children you have, the more difficult it can become.

I realized any past ill-will or disappointment experienced with my mom was unmistakably evident in my relationship with my own daughter. I know Mom has trouble believing my siblings and I have forgiven her for lapses in judgment and how she reared us back when we were kids. But I see it now. I appreciate her better today! I used to worry sometimes about my own daughter's ability to forgive and forget my shortcomings. I am always checking in with Claire who is very protective of me. She sees me striving to be the best mom. Even in my failures, I am not afraid to admit it or to ask her forgiveness. She is my greatest accomplishment. I like asking her, "How am I doing?" I am always rewarded by her reply, "You're doing good! You're cool Mom." I am most proud when I can say, "We are okay!"

For this peace I thank God, and look to my own mother's mistakes, but without hesitation move on because we have a good and healed relationship. I can tell her anything and have learned to appreciate her. Once restored, a greater respect for the precious and tender nature of relationships teaches us to treat them with kindness as they require solid stewardship. As for the past, I knew hardship and appreciate the complexities of our life back then. But now I understand what a mother is supposed to be. Mom was young and raising four children in the seventies; that alone requires a great deal of admiration. My father was also a strained relationship, but a healed one. A witness saw him respond in a way that dumbfounded many. Seeing me at what was likely going to be the end of life, he was overcome with tenderness and grief.

A faithful member of Grace arrived in the ICU on the second day of what I will call "my imprisonment." She and her husband lovingly began to feed the masses. On behalf of the church and at the pastor's request, they delivered pizzas, sandwiches and such. When she entered the hallway outside my room, she saw a man who had been looking at me through a window separating the ICU from hospital turmoil and observers. Bent at the waist and leaning along the wall, he held himself up with one arm secured against the cool glossy tile. Grief stricken, he fell to his knees and wept!

> Moved by this great expression she inquired, "Who's that?"

> "It's my dad," Nancy said. "But I've never seen him act like that."

We try to do our best. But when your child throws your humanity in your face, and reminds you in a not so gentle way you missed the boat--it becomes apparent, "we can't do it [raise godly children, I mean] on our own." It is clear we need supernatural intervention to survive the tests of parenthood. We can only do as much as we know. This situation caused me to call my parents more. I had just learned how to live without them. I had to. But now I feel the need to be closer. I want to be! I need them to know I have forgiven the past. I have been free of all that since I gave my life to Jesus. But for their sakes, I need to be more attentive and share my testimony about what God is doing in my life. My mother also felt there were unresolved issues between us. But sitting bedside and praying I know she found peace. Below are her comments:

At two or three I didn't realize Dina[15] couldn't see. [It is funny how someone with limited eyesight would one day become such a visionary.] It wasn't until I saw her trying to read…she was always reading that child…with the book near the end of her nose, that I sought the help of an optometrist. She began with coke bottle glasses and later wore hard contacts. I had to tell her she was beautiful so she would not be self-conscious. But Adina was not a bad child and sincerely obedient in response to my strict mothering. I raised all my children that way. As a stay at home mother, I needed support. Dina, my oldest daughter, was always very respectful. She began helping with chores around the house and cooking at seven. At the time, I was divorced and living in New York. She escaped the unpleasantness of life by reading. While growing up, there were often problems in the family but we had a fairly open house with lots of kids, cousins, relatives, neighborhood youngsters, anyone who needed help, living with us. It was extremely dysfunctional, but it was home.

The differences between Dina and me are evident. She is a talker, an open, caring and generous person, while I am more demure and laid back. Due to our difficulties we spent a lot of years apart, but I heard she became a Christian, and that she loved her pastor. I was so proud when I heard Dina had become a pastor too.

---

[15] Family nickname for Adina.

I was at work when I first learned she was sick. She'd been ill before, but never in a coma. This was different. She was really on her deathbed, as far as we knew. Nothing would have stopped me from going to her side and her siblings felt the same way. I received a call from my daughter Nancy who filled me in on the details. When I heard the phrase "induced coma,"[16] I caught the next plane.

We arrived in Tucson at the same time. I am glad I'm a saver, so I was able to hop on the next flight out! We all had money and were able to come see my daughter during this critical time. Entering the hospital ICU, we immediately joined Dina at her bed. My son Ricky got upset, Nancy and Rita cried. I was in shock, but no tears. To see her with all the tubes was horrible. I just said, "I am not going to cry, she is in the Lord's hands." I knew all we could do was pray.

Strange to me were all the people lingering in the waiting room. I wondered why everybody was there and what they expected when they saw Dina's family all coming in the door. I have never seen a whole church come together like Grace did. The church family was remarkably good to us too. They set us up in a hotel and brought us food every day. What we witnessed was different; the church was different. Grace family support was extreme and

---

[16] There seems to be a conflict regarding the use of the term "*coma*." Medical records do not support some interview dialogue, such as this one. But we have remained true to the interviewees quoted statements and have left them intact throughout the book.

encouraged me so much. Everyone was very loving and cared so much about her getting well. Alone in the room with Adina, I went back to when she was a little girl, remembering how caring and loving she was and recalling the little things she would do. I prayed for her and held her hand and would kiss her on the cheek. I knew the Lord was going to bring her back. This kind of crisis is not the time to lose your faith, and was definitely not mine. I prayed every day, two or three times per day. I am very thankful for everything He has done for me.

We stayed a couple nights, sleeping in chairs in the ICU. My daughters took care of Adina's hair. I recall Rita saying, "We've got to fix her hair. Nobody's going to see her looking like this." They gave us stuff to wash her hair. We must have washed it three times to get all the blood out. We stayed in Tucson for a whole week and were at the hospital almost every minute, spending most of our time, ten to twelve hours a day, sitting all day. After midnight we returned to our hotel for much needed sleep.

When the kids were younger, they used to go to church. In consideration, I know my kids suffered for the things I did. I remember seeing people in church, standing to testify what great things God had done in their lives. I never felt qualified to speak. Ashamedly I would say to the Lord, "I don't have any reason to testify." I am a very private person and not comfortable talking about the pains of the past. But I always knew I put my kids through five years of torment. I understood they moved on, put it behind them and forgave me, but I never processed those feelings until now. It took the near death of my beloved daughter to force me to examine and express how much I loved all my children. I needed their forgiveness, but even more, I needed to forgive myself. I felt the Lord say to me, "You really need something to testify!" While she was lying there, I realized I had to speak about what a miracle God would do in her life. As well, I was certain Dina didn't realize how much I loved her because I had done so many things for which I felt guilty. I prayed to the Lord, "Please don't take her from me." I didn't think Dina knew how much I loved her cause I never told her.

Reconciliation occurred between mother and daughter, but also between my mother and her God. This was an answer to years of prayer. As a mother myself, I understand being a mom is hard and at times we fail. In the process, those failures hurt our children. How we wish we could take those things back, get a do over so no scars remain. But now as a mother, I understand my mom's role even better. We put our moms on pedestals they cannot possibly maintain. Knowing this, the Lord allows us to see our mothers for who they really are and love them in an even greater capacity. In spite of the inevitable disappointments, we can still appreciate mothers for their sacrifices, efforts, and energies; they are after all super heroes. Right?

A Mother's Heart

It was suggested the knowledge I had to make it on my own at such an early age is what hurts my mom. I was forced to be independent of family to become the woman I am today in my own way. For Claire I want to fill the void, every empty place. I understand what the confusion of emerging womanhood feels like, and I do not want her to go that road alone, but prefer to gently guide her through the mine field that life and all its drama can bequeath to innocent young people. Like all good parents, I want her pursuits to be greater, bigger, better than mine, and I know she can and will do it.

Claire entered her teens. I admit this was more traumatizing for me. The transition between childhood and womanhood is not an easy metamorphosis, especially when admittance begins with a dying mother. Watching television with her dad and family Trevor showed up and mentioned rather casually, according to Claire, that "her mom was in intensive care."

Trevor said during all the madness his thoughts turned to the other lady in his life, his stepdaughter:

> I wrestled with how I was going to tell Claire about her mom, and I worried whether or not she would continue to be a part of my life should something awful happen.

A phone call seemed inadequate, so he drove over to her dad's house and knocked on the door. Claire's father answered. Trevor communicated about the emergency room ordeal and assured her God was in control. *Philippians 4:7* talks about "God's peace which passes understanding," and Trevor shared the peace and presence of the Lord with Claire and her paternal family. "We will get more information to you as soon as possible," Trevor said. "All we know is that she ate pineapple and now she's in the hospital."

Claire noticed Trevor was not acting normally, wringing his hands while extremely anxious. He looked really tired, and she knew it must be bad or else he would have just called and told her over the phone. Tearing up, she decided not to go the hospital at that time.

After school on Tuesday, Nancy, Rita, Ricky and Mom picked her up and took her to the surgery waiting area. My mom and siblings agreed it was pivotal Claire come, and if necessary, say good-bye. She knew I was really sick. They all felt she was intelligent and developed enough to handle what would at least be **shocking**. They sat with her as she readied herself, bracing for what I would look like. They wanted to be sure she was equipped. Nancy, the take-charge *Nurse Ratchet*[17] of the family, and my baby sister along with the support of others, tried to paint a picture. My eyes were patched shut, a tube in my mouth to help me breathe, gauze wrapped around my head, mouth, throat, and a towel draped across my forehead, monitors measuring my life, and eight intravenous tubes running in and out of my body, forcing fluids, medication, antibiotics, and sedatives used to keep me paralyzed, and unconscious. Nancy spoke to her like a momma, stepping into my role with loving and tender words and a kindly forbearance. The idea was to avoid frightening Claire when she saw all the crazy critical life-saving steps. Although optimism was on their minds, death was looming. Claire assures me, she never had doubts her mother, the mighty Christian warrior— the woman she had grown up with -- would succumb to anything as harmless as a piece of pineapple. Already 13, she was no longer a child per se, and was in the age of accountability and responsible for what she knows. Spiritual things are a reality to her. Although she will always be under my mothering mantle, my protection, my covering, I am impressed with her discernment and maturity. She is becoming an independent and confident woman. "You go Claire!" Trevor also had a unique perspective on what God was doing within the family:

> It was amazing to see God at work. Not just with
> my wife, but in every aspect of life. One of the most
> notable evidences of God's sovereign involvement in

---

[17] A fictional character from the 1962 novel, "One Flew Over the Cuckoo's Nest," whose reputation was one of strict adherence to the establishment and unyielding order in a mental care environment.

our lives was when I realized just about every single damaged relationship, be it family, friend or foe, started a process of reconciliation. I had a chance to speak with Sam, my father-in-law. I know that conversation meant a lot to both of us. My family, her family and a lot of friends and other people in our spheres of influence had a chance to talk things out. Nothing unifies like a common enemy and when this tragedy struck, all of the things separating us just seemed so trivial. For example, to say that there has been tension between Adina and Claire's dad is an understatement. When I informed him about Adina, something changed. It was no longer us over here and them over there. We began to communicate about Adina and to coordinate Claire's visitations. He and his wife even invited me and the rest of Adina's family over for dinner. We went and had a great time. It was a nice change of pace from the gloomy scenery at the hospital, and was an extremely encouraging time. It almost seemed the worse Adina's situation grew, the more hope, mercy, and grace was pumped into every conversation.

Our Heritage

My story is filled with many miraculous moments, but none quite as unusual as the reconciliation of my daughter's family with mine. God does work in all the details. On Friday, February 10th, the Jewish *Sabbath* occurred. The meal known as *Shabbat* (meaning a ceasing or stopping of the day's activities -- the seventh day -- for the purpose of rest) was a time the families shared together. Orthodox Jews do this every Friday at sundown. Although not orthodox, Claire's paternal family does observe this holy day, and on this occasion invited my mother, husband and siblings over to join them and Claire in celebration.

The **Shabbat** features drinking wine and eating **Challah bread**. Specific prayers are spoken over the wine, bread and candles. At the end of the meal, the diners will traditionally pound on the table with their fists symbolizing, "Thank you God!" Every family has their own expression of Shabbat, but the ritual commemorates the time when Israelites wandered in the desert for forty years after their exodus from Egypt, and where *manna* fell from heaven. Manna did not fall on the *Sabbath* or holidays. Instead, a double portion would fall before any celebration. Hence, Hebrews gathered enough provisions for two days.

The meal is a time of fellowship, family, laughter and storytelling. You enter Shabbat when the women light candles representing the family. Then the Friday night meal begins with a blessing over the wine. **Kiddush** is shared; everyone has their own cup of wine and a prayer is spoken. The invocation sounds something like: *Praise to You, Adonai our God, Sovereign of the universe, Creator of the fruit of the vine.* Afterwards, Challah bread is served. Each single loaf is woven with six strands. The meal includes two loaves representing the twelve tribes of Israel. *HaMotzi* is a prayer spoken over the bread. Words of the blessing communicate glory to God and thankfulness for the bread: *Blessed are You, Adonai our God, Ruler of the universe, who brings forth bread from the earth.* More prayers are spoken throughout the *Shabbat* celebration as prayers, thanksgiving, and remembrance are keys to the festivities.

Trevor noticed Claire was happy. She was showing everyone her room and sharing with them the details of her life. Having her family together in one place, experiencing one amazing moment was a twinkle of joy in the midst of great sorrow. My prayer now is that, against all odds, our families will press through and continue to build relationships. Even though God moves in miraculous ways, so often in family situations, we fail to acknowledge the inexplicable and the relationships begin to wane. It breaks my heart, but not my faith. I believe God can and is still working in all of our lives.[v]

> During the meal, it was Nancy who commented about the supernatural nature of the shared meal. She looked around the room as everyone was talking and said, "God is good. This isn't about Adina. It's bigger than that." Family is never more real than during times when sharing a difficult journey!

> Trevor added, "It was as if God put His hand on my shoulder and literally walked us through all of this. I know He is our Comforter and Counselor, but I have never experienced His closeness to this extent."

It is my prayer, a dream actually, that involves this kind of renewed relational healing where ***family wholeness*** is not a temporary response to the incredible circumstances we all labored under. It grieves me to think we could not continue to walk in mutual love for the sake of Claire. I know the strain this kind of discord put her under. Lack of freedom to freely talk about her family and to share time together does not respect the role, function, purpose, and necessity of family. Although I would have preferred to be there celebrating with them, my mother's heart is filled with joy at the thought of such a wholly surprising reconciliation.

Friends

Ministry experiences have allowed multiple opportunities to meet and befriend some amazing Christians. Although there were many brothers in the faith who stepped-up and contended in the Spirit and played an extensive role in my healing, this section focuses on a list of exceptional females who are also a part of my special family. Here are a few notes about some whom I feel especially close. Jacque R as previously mentioned is one of my dearest and closest friends. We have known each other for roughly twenty-seven years. And believe me when I say, we have shared everything. "She is my *sista*[18] and we speak the same language." I can see her across the room and know if she is feeling sad, mad, happy or glad. And she is the same with me. We share a long illustrious history that involves our BC (before Christ) lives. In lieu of all our time together, we experienced a lot of shared joy and sorrow, sin and repentance. Many emotional altars marking our journey have passed between us.

Jacque was surely one of those most devastated by my situation. Our backstory is the underpinning of our sisterhood. Even before becoming a pastor, I was always encouraging and counseling others. A mutual friend called at five in the morning asking counsel for someone in crisis over an ended relationship. So I picked up my phone and gave her a call.

> "Hey Girl, I hear you are going through some girl drama. Let me tell you one of my break-up stories."

> I talked about things I have walked through so she would understand she was not alone. By the end of the three-hour conversation, we were both laughing and I asked, "Are you gonna' be okay?"

> "Yeah, I think so," she said

> "If you need anything, you can call."

But instead of waiting for her call, I just started to call her. This continued for months before we ever met. We would talk almost every day about everything and anything: life, men, jobs, relationships.

---

[18] A slang term for the word *sister* which is pronounced "sistah."

We finally met face to face when she called me one night and asked, "Hey, what are you doing?"

"I'm going out," I said. "But I can't find my belt."

"Oh, I'll bring you one," she said.

"Great!"

She came to my place with a black leather belt size one (I wore size seven). I looked at the belt, hanging it by the buckle, dangling it over my head and said, "Is this a headband? This thing is so tiny, it will never fit! It's like bringing a knife to a gun fight. Are you joking?"

We laughed about it, thereby cementing our friendship in the process. Jacque keeps me real. The Christian life can be really lonely sometimes because everything is always changing. We came to Grace through different circumstances, but sharing our growth in the things of God has always been reassuring. She insists she never lost hope or faith in recovery.

> "Adina always said, 'It's not my time.' Even when the doctors implied she would probably not make it, I knew she would, because she still had so much to do in this life," says Jacque.

The final segment in my family album would have to include my Pastor and friend Rae, (which is discussed elsewhere in this book), and my spiritual mother and friend, Reverend LaNora Morin.

The first time I encountered LaNora (formerly Van Arsdall) was at a Tucson prayer meeting called "Praise at the Gates." I was introduced then blown away by her strength and knowledge of the Word. Roughly a month later I heard her speak at a women's conference she hosted in the Phoenix area. A friend encouraged me to come and hear this amazing prophet who moved in spiritual things, commanding authority like few do. Since I was not expecting to have a life altering encounter, I did not commit any details to memory. Only in the aftermath did I stand amazed at how divinely God works in our day-to-day circumstances. Powerful in principle, LaNora, though small in stature (if she is 5'1"--it's too tall) had to stand on a platform so those of us in the back of the church could see her. Though petite, she is huge in the Word and the things of God. So amazing!"

An infant in spiritual truths at the time, the message she spoke was not remembered, but yet unforgettable. I was in awe! While listening to her words, I heard the Lord say: "Where she goes, you will go, and her people will be your people and her God will be your god," a verse from the book of Ruth,[19] which I had no idea was in the Bible. At this point, I had not even read the Word all the way through and had no concept of Ruth and her amazing, yet vaguely similar journey.

Afterwards, I approached LaNora for an introduction. I remember she had just finished ministering, bodies everywhere, *slain in the Spirit*, as she sat down in the afterglow of the Holy Spirit next to her armor-bearer and good friend Barb. With a great deal of anxiety, I went to tell her the good news. I was so scared to say what the Lord had revealed. How do you tell someone, "Congratulations, it's a girl!" At the time, I did not have a good relationship with my own mother, so this meant a lot to me. Besides, her two daughters were there also, so I am sure they were all thrilled at the prospect of their newest family member.

Scared to death and draped in tears, my voice shaking I said, "The Lord told me you're to be my mother. I sat on my knees in front of her and began to pour out my heart. Suddenly another

---

[19] Referencing Ruth 1:16.

woman came alongside me and announced the same incredible thing. LaNora, who experiences these sorts of declarations on a nearly daily basis, was very matter-of-fact when she said, "We'll see!" The smile on her face was kind, but full of wisdom, implying all would be revealed in time. I started calling her "Mother LaNora" after the Lord spoke to me about her becoming my spiritual mom. It's a name that stuck.

There is nothing she would not do for me. A mother will speak truth into your life whether or not you want to hear it. She was at my wedding and I just remember her standing there. Not only did she have a new daughter, but she accepted and embraced a new son. Mother LaNora will have many other daughters and sons, but I know Trevor and I are the real deal. We are committed to her and her calling, her family and her purpose. We will go to any length and do whatever she requires…this truth is what makes her family. We have gone on trips to Israel together and shared many other experiences, like breaking bread, praying for one another and worshipping. When she married Jody, I gained a new papa. He is lovingly called Papa Jody and has become a role model to us. Although not a natural birth, still she loves me, teaches, disciplines, and equips me for a spiritual walk, while protecting, and aiding me to become a competent minster of the gospel. She helps me grow-up in the things of God, always demonstrating duties associated with motherhood. It is hard to describe that kind of love. All her efforts exhibit what being a part of the family of God truly means!

These multiplied relationships have added to the rich texture of my family's tapestry. The experiences have sealed and joined us into an intricate combination of pictures depicting our greater lineage. Family connection is so powerful!

CHAPTER FIVE

Do The Sick No Harm

... there should be no schism in the
body; but that the members should have
the same care one for another.
1 Corinthians 12:25 (KJV)

Hospital Stay

As the saying goes, a cat has nine lives. During those first days of recovery it seemed mine was redeemed over and over again. It would be nine days before people witnessed signs of returning to normal life.[20] Nurses and the anesthesiologist said I died at least twice. I was eager to learn specifics. Pulling together the cacophony of professionals weighing-in on what happened, and finding ways to consolidate all details into one voice was no small task.

There were primarily five physicians who cared for me, three willing and available for interviews. But before we examine those conversations, I want to say for the sake of this story, there is no

---

[20] First demonstrated cognitive behavior was on the eighth day following incident. On the ninth day, I began doing things like communicating with others beyond what doctors expected.

criticism or culpability being implied, validated or disproven through anyone's testimony. I am alive, which says a lot about the care I received. But I must add it was spiritual intervention that saved my life. Still, the doctors, nurses, and support staff, who performed valiantly in their rescue efforts, are angels who worked to save me from imminent death. Gratitude best describes my thoughts regarding them.

Dr. Fredy T stayed with me until I went into surgery. Dr. Robert D performed corrective surgery and ultimately saved my life, while Dr. Hannah D was the anesthesiologist, and Dr. David T was commissioned with caring for my brain after surgery. A fifth physician provided emotional and mental support as I was recuperating. Three professional men and two women whose dedication brought me through what no one thought possible. God used mighty specialists to bring me back to a life that was able to begin almost where I left off with only minor adjustments that are still being revealed. Like a convoluted puzzle, the brain is not one size fits all! I awake each day with expectancy, always trusting the Lord will sustain me. The crisis which seems so far away now, is only a blip on my lifeline. In spite of evidence indicating I would be either severely limited or mentally challenged, I survived. Unimaginable is the thought I could ever forget these heroes or their epic efforts.

Medical Madness

Anoxic injury, also known as *hypoxia*, a physical disturbance caused by abnormally low amounts of oxygen in the body tissue, was the germinating point of all the medical commotion. Recovery prospect was bleak. Tasks performed by doctors are best shared in their own words. Breaking it all down, there are questions about what happened, how I ended up in the hospital, and what steps were taken to save my life. Allowing the physicians to speak for themselves, we have quoted them as much as possible to convey the details and oftentimes confusion of that ill-fated day. Accessing a severe case of anaphylaxis, Dr. David T explained:

She had an allergic reaction to pineapple which caused her throat to shut so she was incapable of breathing; a pretty shocking example. This was the most severe case where I had a person as young as her whose airway closed. Such cases are not super common, but these episodes kill people. Swelling was so severe the airway tightened so no oxygen could get in requiring a trach;[21] a very dangerous position to be in.

Following emergency transport to the hospital, EMTs are required to do what is called *a transfer of custody*,[22] thereby placing patient into the physician's capable hands. Unfortunately, my arrival did not go as smoothly as one would hope. I ended up in the emergency bay where another rather horrendous episode occurred (a detailed account follows later).

"Her lungs looked like a bag with all the air removed, completely shut down," said Anesthesiologist Dr. Hannah D. On day-call, Dr. Hannah finished all scheduled surgeries and was heading home when a call requesting return to surgery altered her plans.

"Dr. D has a patient with a tracheostomy,"[23] said the operator.

---

[21] Abbreviation for terms "tracheostomy" and "tracheotomy."

[22] *Transfer of custody* means the EMT must hand the patient over to the care of a doctor. At the time of the incident, procedure dictated EMTs could not deliver patient to ER, then leave without a qualified physician present.

[23] Tracheostomy and tracheotomy are terms often used interchangeably. *Tracheostomy* is the surgical construction of an artificial opening in the trachea, while *tracheotomy* refers to an incision in the trachea.

That was all the information given. Ten minutes later she was changing into scrubs. Emergency prep involves careful sterilization, but due to the critical situation, Dr. Hannah haphazardly slopped soap on her hands, a perfunctory cleanse before joining the surgeon, who was taking measures to repair the trachea wound in my neck Directed by a single digit waved in the air, she headed to the ER bay to assess the situation. Anesthesiologists are physicians specializing in the management of physical sensation or pain during surgery. Using drugs or gas, they sedate the patient. They also perform perioperative care developing patient specific plans. In a flash, Dr. Hannah made decisions that would affect recovery.

> "Adina didn't look so hot," Dr. Hannah said. With the tracheal tube placed in her neck, I had to get an oxygen reading. Saturation was fifty to sixty percent, consistent with anaphylaxis."

> Normal oxygen saturation for someone on ventilation should be between ninety to one-hundred percent. Told she had experienced cardiac arrest in the field, "I was unable to draw any conclusions on her chance of survival, but if asked, I would have said fifty-fifty." Taking control of ventilation, her primary focus was to control the bagging of my airway during surgery.

> "Sometimes you can feel the elasticity in someone's lungs," Dr. Hannah said. "Bronchia spasm, the tightening up and closing down of the airway, was felt right away. Basically this meant no air was getting into her lungs." Then she added, "Adina, who was treated with epinephrine, was very swollen most

likely from the anaphylaxis. Facial swelling made it
difficult to insert the airway tube into her mouth."

Also contacted to join the arena of medical support was on-call surgeon Dr. Robert D. Summoned to ER **stat** (doctor lingo for *immediately*) to what he described as a "panic situation" for an emergency rescue. He changed clothes and drove to the hospital. "I knew it was urgent and they were going to need my help."

Dr. Robert D, an ENT Otolaryngology, arrived on the scene to repair damage done to my neck. After roughly eighteen years education and residency, and seventeen-plus years of experience, he is often called to work under intense pressure while performing some pretty high-risk procedures. Dr. McDreamy, as he is affectionately called by admirers, demonstrated great attention to detail, an obvious asset in performing delicate surgery.

> "The airway had been secured but they could not figure out why she was bleeding," Dr. Robert said. "With such excessive blood flow it was hard to determine the source, so it was necessary to clamp off vessels to determine injury severity." He further added: My first gut instinct was dismal as a presumptively compromised airway made the situation critical. Adina had not been medically sedated [when surgery began]. Unconscious since ambulance transport and due to all that transpired before surgery, sedation was not necessary.

When I first encountered Dr. Robert, of course, I was totally unconscious and hemorrhaging. He describes his remedial steps and diagnosis:

I took her to the operating room, tried to control the bleeding, pulled out the tracheostomy tube in her neck, inspected her tracheal wall and removed excessive tissue, all while exploring the bleeding source. Later I closed the wound. My interactions after that were to check her wounds and vitals to watch her from minute to minute to observe such things as when she opened her eyes or moved her extremities. She continued to show improvement. I was impressed with her tenacity.

Review of medical team decisions reveal seemingly solid rationales for choices made during a time of unknown outcomes and no guarantees. Dr. Hannah explains her curative actions:

Due to instability, I did not have her under deep anesthesia for two reasons. Light, general anesthesia is recommended in the case of unstable vital signs. And due to her low oxygen levels, I could not get "gas" (the type of anesthesia used) into her airway. Upon completion of surgery, Adina's oxygen saturation level was stable and in the nineties.

According to Dr. Hannah, toward the end of surgery it is standard protocol to give a patient generic medication to prevent surgery recall. Midazolam (a distant cousin to Valium) was injected into an IV to promote memory loss for the one to two hours immediately surrounding the operation. Stabilized vital signs indicate patient's recuperation; now it was time to mend. Dr. David T came to see me two days later. A leader in southern Arizona's neurological community with emphasis on stroke victims, Dr. David modestly confessed, "I hate to overstate my importance or credentials." He recommended treatment that included therapeutic cooling of my body to safeguard the brain's integrity. The treatment approach is simple: cool somebody down to reduce their metabolic rate, thus preventing organs from shutting down completely.

Neurologists specialize in investigation, diagnosis, and treatment of neurological disorders. As the Director of Stroke and Division Chair of Urology, a position held for five years (at the time of the incident), Dr. David was called-in as an expert to help determine a post-operative care strategy. Related to the human nervous system, neurology encompasses the brain, spinal cord, peripheral nerves, and diseases affecting them. After assessing the potential brain damage caused by an extended lack of oxygen, the doctor devised a plan to stabilize and facilitate healing.

"I was called in to assess and determine if there was any brain function, assess the patient and give a neurological evaluation," Dr. David said. Examination determined lack of oxygen results and what kind of anoxic injury I had sustained. He was concerned the trauma damaged me in ways yet to be discovered.

Days of Uncertainty

Sunday was truly a dark time, and the following day was much the same. Monday brought more tears, prayers, friends, and family to commiserate together as I lay motionless. Trevor spent most of the day talking with doctors, on the phone, and speaking with people who came to show their support. He had little sleep and hardly left the hospital, but noted the cafeteria had surprisingly good food. Coming from a former professional chef, that is saying something. In the early morning, he stole away for a couple of hours to pray and seek the Lord. "Time away gave me a chance to clear my head, pour out my heart and strengthen myself," Trevor added.

Post-surgery, hospital days were anything but ordinary. Chaos best describes the daily routine in any intensive care unit. Trevor, whose constant and unwavering presence, witnessed and participated in every moment, decision and victory, reflects on those early days:

I finally had a chance to be alone with my wife. All the tubes, bandages, and machines were overwhelming. I later learned during her intake and while trying to get her airway open, she breathed in a lot of blood. Tears and prayers flowed, pastors and friends stayed with me late into the night. I attempted to make myself comfortable in the waiting room, but to no avail. I did not get any sleep with the make-shift bed-chair while the horrific images of the day replayed again and again.

Trevor said hospital techs were phenomenal. Two nurses in particular were like pit bulls, guard dogs, very protective, taking care of me like I was their own. Let me say whoever you are, "thank you." All staff voiced disgust at what happened to an ordinarily healthy woman now clinging to life. Everyone agreed my situation was such a disservice, and were genuinely concerned about the loss of an otherwise normal lifecycle.

By Tuesday the waiting room was full of visitors. In traditional Grace to the Nations style, a make shift buffet was erected. Trevor said, "The almost paralyzing feeling of helplessness was stayed with prayer and pasta." He also noted "at least fifty times" many different caring and concerned faces would present themselves, however gingerly, and question how he was doing, inquiring about ways to help:

"What can I do to help, Trevor?"

"Pray," he would say in a rather impassioned but even-keeled tone.

"You need to eat," they would declare, then add, "I'll bring you something."

Despite his responses, they would return with a home cooked something or other for everyone to share. But food and rest were the least of Trevor's concerns.

On Wednesday Trevor met Dr. David T who explained because of the level of sedation, it would be impossible to determine anything regarding brain wave activity. Plans were already underway to return body temperature to normal following the use of an appliance to cool the body. Nursing staff applied electrolyzed pads wrapped like bandages around each leg to increase circulation preventing blood clots. All efforts were made in hopes I would regain consciousness. He assured Trevor, due to length of time without oxygen, I **had** suffered brain damage. To what extent was the question? He explained:

> It may be she can't walk or speak ever again, may require admission to a rehabilitation center, or it may be she can walk and do most of the things she used to do, but will talk a little slower. Either way I want you to know she's going to be different.

Furthermore, Trevor was warned this was an extremely critical time, as the warming procedure can provoke many complications. Of course the grim discussion regarding a living will, resuscitation, or life support brought on a whole new surge of emotions. Another wave of intercession and more tears as Trevor contacted key people in charge of distributing prayer requests.

In a rather poignant moment, Trevor spent a couple hours talking to and praying over me. During that time, a rather amusing moment was shared.

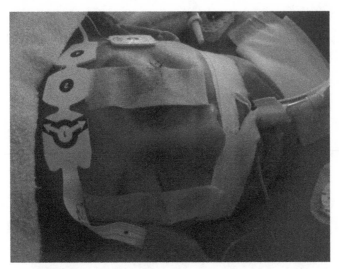

PHOTO 5-1: Adina hooked to machines measuring
brain waves and monitoring brain activity.

Usually not one for comic relief, Adina would later
laugh at what happened next. If you know anything
about her, you know she is a fighter! She is definitely
someone you want for you and not against you. She
was being chemically sedated and paralyzed. I told
her they were going to warm her up and that the
next twenty-four hours were critical. I whispered
in her ear, "It's time to fight." Just then the screen
reflecting the heart monitor showed an arrhythmia
(a disturbance in the regular heartbeat). The marker
shot up, the warning bell sounded and the nurse
came running. Adina's sedatives were adjusted
to maintain proper distribution of medication. I
chuckled and responded, "Ok, allow me to correct
that last statement. You just rest and heal. Let us
fight for you." With that she relaxed.

Meanwhile, doctors witnessed improvement, but did not want to be overly optimistic either. While I secretly moved towards wellness, Trevor pushed to the edge of total exertion:

> Due to lack of sleep, I was fairly stressed out. I was beginning to feel the pressure from taking and making more phone calls, coordinating prayer points and updates, speaking with and escorting people to her hospital bed, not to mention all the ongoing meetings with doctors and discussions with hospital crew.
>
> What grieved me most was I had not heard my wife's voice or even seen her move for going on four days. Adina's sisters assured me they would keep watch over her and would call immediately if there were any new developments. Finally I got some sleep; not a lot, but enough to keep me sane.
>
> I woke up Thursday morning and immediately went to prayer. Presenting myself before the Lord, I said, "Okay Lord, its day five and I have no idea what today is going to bring, but here I am. I trust You!" I was about to walk out the door and head to the hospital, but stopped. I was weary and needed to strengthen myself in the Lord. I picked up my guitar and prepared my heart to worship. Adina and I have prayed and worshipped as I played the guitar many times. One of our favorite songs is "You Are My King (Amazing Love)." As I began to play, I could feel the comfort of the Lord wash over me. As I hit the chorus, I could hear Adina's voice harmonizing with mine. I broke down in tears and

continued to play and to my amazement, I could still hear her voice. God is so good! He always gives us what we need. This journey was like climbing up a mile-high ladder. I couldn't see the top or bottom and right when I felt like I was going to fall, He placed the next rung in my hand and stabilized my footing.

With the care of family, hospital personnel worked tirelessly to help me on the recovery road. But so much of what happened was truly the Lord's intervention.

Challenging Status Quo

The human brain is central to existence, but experts agree medical research has not been able to tap into the complexity of how the brain functions. While much is known about the human body, some experts assert less than .01% is understood about the human mind. Believers often refer to the mind as the **soul**: the place where we store personality, our will, cognition, intelligence, feelings and emotions. When it comes to higher level functioning, meaning spiritual knowledge, even less is truly understood about the brain. Generally, doctors do not comprehend the spiritual side of the healing work they perform on the body. Only God can heal the mind. Even experts admit they do not understand, nor can they explain remarkable feats only possible with godly intervention.[vi]

During the unconscious state it is impossible to prove with absolute medical certainty what is going on in the mind of the patient. What I saw, felt or recognized cannot be verified either. The brain's reaction and related information is enigmatic. In fact, experts reaffirmed it is unfeasible to be conscious of what happens around a patient in the hospital while sedated. Doctors also suggested, in my case, it would be highly unlikely to dream. Confidently, I can affirm that God was responsible for restoring my frontal cortex to normal function. For me it is the only plausible explanation!

The care plan involved icing the body to reduce core body temperature to put all major functions to sleep by strategically chilling all extremities. I was literally packed in ice to prevent the organs from shutting down. The American Anesthesiology website says this kind of sedation is used "… to form…an induced blunting of consciousness…it also affects response to external stimulation." The fact I was physically moving during such times was intriguing. One doctor later told me my behavior was abnormal because I kept fighting. It seemed as if my spirit was ruling the body, when in fact during sedation, this is also considered unachievable. Medical records - and there sure are a lot of them - are supposedly produced for every MRI, EKG, even every blood draw. Medical staff is charged with writing observations in reports listing procedural details and noting anything unusual. Spending on average one-third of their time in paperwork recording all activity associated with patient care makes medicine an even more complex and meticulous job. By this time, medical staff thought I may have contracted MRSA (Methicillin-resistant Staphylococcus aureus). MRSA is an often hospital-related bacterium responsible for several difficult-to-treat human infections. MRSA's introduction can greatly complicate any patient's ability to recover. As a result, everyone had to wear gloves and a gown adding complicated calisthenics to the hospital's already exacting procedures. Trevor was particularly disturbed by this latest development. "It was bad enough she was even in the hospital, and I could not speak to her, but now I could not touch her," he lamented.

Through the next few days they ran test after test and took multiple x-rays. When talking to Dr. David, he mentioned my base brain functions, those controlling my organs and involuntary reactions, seemed to be intact. But he also cautioned Trevor, "She may not remember who you are, but already she is doing much better than expected." They conducted a sensory reflex test agitating the patient by running the tip of a pen up and down the foot. Apparently, I reacted and pulled away. But Trevor was told not to have false hope as these were "reflective and not purposeful responses," which meant my nervous system was reacting to stimuli and not because I chose to cognitively engage.

Thursday, February 9th, the doctors attempted to bring me out of the medically induced paralysis they anticipated would save my life. In typical *Adina fashion,* I came out of paralysis with my arms and legs flailing. In Christian circles, I have been identified as a fighter. These words describe life prior to becoming a Christian. Basically, I was confrontational! But as a believer, I became a fighter for God and my natural instinct turned toward heavenly war. "From the days of John the Baptist until now, the kingdom of heaven has suffered violence, and the violent take it by force" *Matthew 11:12 (ESV).* I truly appreciate this scripture and believe it embodies my Christian philosophy, while fully explaining my oftentimes unusual passion for godly matters. Due to the amount of sedation, doctors said it would be impossible for a patient to maneuver their extremities or control their limbs, but I had to be restrained to prevent from hurting myself. Go figure! Little by little, I began the fight to return to myself. Trevor interpreted what he witnessed:

> As the sedatives wore off, her eyes opened. Over the course of the next two days, her movements were very mechanical. She looked almost animatronic. At first I was so excited, but when I looked into her eyes she wasn't there. She made the same repetitive movements. Her eyes would open and scan from left to right and then close. Next time she would do the same, but add a head turn. It seemed as though her brain was rebooting. This was hard for me to watch. Looking into my wife's eyes and knowing she was not there.

Tragic! I comforted myself with the analogy that her brain is like a computer rebooting after a crash. What I witnessed was Adina resetting and reloading.

Revival

While everyone prayed, Dr. David T began the arduous task of bringing me out of unconsciousness. He explains benchmarks in this process:

> Cooling the body caused routine functions to slow down the consumption of energy; thereby allowing preservation of areas that otherwise might have been lost. Initially she had quite a bit of medication still in her. The next day, she still wasn't responding. She wasn't following my commands; she looked but had no response. She appeared frozen. The second day I saw her was February 7th, at 10:45 p.m.. I witnessed beginning efforts to rewarm her body. Rating her recovery, I thought she was in the three or four range out of ten, with one being bad and ten being good. I was cautiously hopeful, but I was definitely on the side of *this doesn't look good!*

> I needed to establish degree of injury to the brain to determine if she would survive, and to ascertain whether or not she would be in a persistent vegetative state. It is hard to predict results with any certainty. Prognosis was a **gray zone** and not favorable. I feared she would not come out of the drug induced coma quite right. During this ordeal she sustained a couple small strokes. But everything else looked okay. By February 11th and 12th, she started following commands. She made quite a remarkable turnaround. And she clearly

looked great on February 13th, and again on the 16th. Concerned she might stay in a gray area, I was pleased to witness how rapidly things started to change. But the brain kind of does that stuff. We really don't have a great grasp of how to predict what will happen in this set of patients. Behavior and medical conditions are hard to interpret when talking about the brain. It is difficult to know for certain what will happen in the future. We knew the longer her progress took would be a bad indicator. It was impressive how quickly she got better. When I came back she was doing everything I asked her to do, and was quite alert.

The ambiguity associated with brain-related injuries far outweighs what doctors know and can predict about trauma patient aftermath. Rather than medical miracles, the outcomes really are heaven sent and mystery bound. There were other real moments of joy in spite of negative elements. Trevor talks about when we first made eye contact. He said, "I thought I would collapse under the waves of relief and joy the first time she squeezed my hand and nodded in affirmation to a question I asked." Trevor describes what happened:

> While spending another tender moment with Adina, she demonstrated a cycle of mechanical repetitive movement. I held her hand, kissed it and told her I loved her. As her eyes scanned back and forth, they stopped and met mine. It was as if she looked directly into my soul. There she was, my Adina! Then for a brief moment I saw her eyes moisten and brighten. She looked right at me and cracked a smile. I moved my head from side to side and she followed. After about thirty seconds her eyes closed and she fell back

asleep. It took a lot out of her, but Adina was present. I tear up all over again remembering that special moment. Our prayers preceded breakthrough, and hopefully, my wife was back.

To check her awareness and ability to respond, whoever was in the room repeatedly asked her to squeeze their hand. Up to this point she was unresponsive. Her brother Ricky, someone she had been through a lot with and whom she shared a special bond, grabbed her arm, picked it up and dropped it. He did this a couple of times. I was getting angry and about to stop him when I decided to watch instead. He moved down to her feet and repeatedly lightly smacked them.

"You don't like this do you?" he said. "Well, then do something about it!"

In typical brotherly fashion, he repeated these oddly familiar actions over and over while agitating her in the process. Suddenly, she pulled her arm away. She moved her leg and squeezed my hand. I could tell by her eyes she was cognizant and likely a little angry.

Tearfully I asked, "Can you hear me? If so, blink twice."

She blinked, twice!

"I'm going to ask you a question to find out where you're at." I paused for a moment then probed, "Is my name Bill?"

With wrinkled nose in an all-too common quirky expression, she shot me a familiar look that verbalized, "Are you kidding me?" Immediately I knew she was going to be okay. For the first time since this whole thing began, I felt as if we were out of the woods. Now we needed to focus on our hospital exit.

It was an excruciatingly painful time as I saw my wife lay motionless for almost a week. It was also an amazingly beautiful time of being with the Lord as He helped me navigate life's storm. He is near the brokenhearted. Adina was in the hospital for a total of thirteen days, and in that time I got to see miracles all around me: in my wife, friends, family, and even broken relationships He restored. When they finally removed the breathing tube and I heard her voice, an intense feeling of peace and love swelled within. We spoke, prayed, counted our blessings and cried.

Our marriage was strong (still is), but all couples have times where they are challenged to work things out. The relational healing between Trevor and me was a glimpse of the kinds of relationships God was moving to restore in our lives. Although it has been mentioned before, we underwent many estranged friendships and family connections which were miraculously reunited during the hospitalization and following recovery time at home. I can only marvel at God's miraculous ways and healing powers. I saw Him reworking so many of the broken associations during this season. It is my prayer every person on the planet one day experiences how special it is when God intervenes in your afflicted relationships. It was such a healing, refreshing and regenerating time of hope! Recovering was the least of my worries when I first came out of the drug induced paralysis. It would be several days before I was truly cognizant of people and my surroundings.

Wedding Bells

When I opened my eyes on the tenth, I was officially declared "conscious." But I have no recollection or memories of what transpired in those first few days. Wedding plans were originally in the works for Jacque and her fiancé Ulysses to marry on February 12, 2012. And of course, I was supposed to be the matron-of-honor, but the incident changed all that. Up to this point, Jacque had laid her plans down. Her thoughts were, "How can I get married when my best friend is in ICU?" Upon my awakening, she declared, "Adina's awake! Let's get married." Like soldiers in WWII who married their sweethearts, then immediately left for war, the value of sharing the experience was so much more important than the ideal of a church wedding. Our devotion to each other is one reason Jacque wanted to celebrate her nuptials in the intensive care unit. And as odd as it seems, we did!

I suppose her rush was due in part to the instability of my condition. Afraid I might fail to revive; she wanted to be sure to include me, photos and all, in her wedding day. So on February 12th, her simple ceremony was held in the hospital Intensive Care Unit, right next to my bed. Pastors Obed and Rae officiated. Sadly, I do not recall any of the ceremony. But I am told, and photographs and video verify, I was happy to be there!

PHOTO 5-2: Wedding Day. (From left to right): Alyssa, Ulysses, and Jacque C.

Conceptually Conscious

As a pastor I have been to countless ICUs where people are sick and dying and it is so often a solemn and morbid experience because people are in life threatening situations. There is no joy! But on Valentine's Day, there were balloons, teddy bears, flowers, laughter, music and friends. There was so much joy, unheard of in an ICU. I think that is why they kept telling us, however kindly spoken, "Be quiet!" A party atmosphere in the ICU is another oddity, but that is the very definition of miraculous.

Because the breathing tube taped to my mouth had not yet been removed, conversation was impossible. But by the second week I was demonstrating cognition. I asked for a clipboard and paper so I could communicate with others. Dr. David T noted what he described as nearly instantaneous change. "When she woke up, BOOM, she woke up," he said.

Brighter Days

In spite of a dismal atmosphere there were growing instances of joy and hope of cheerier days ahead. One positive was the warm blankets--literally stored in warming ovens. Warm blanket moments were the best; like chocolate chip cookies or grandma. The warm covering provided comfort contrasting the ceaseless cold of every hospital I have ever been in. The unsympathetic environment echoes the detachment of the hospital experience, someone else's pain, some other person's loss. But unanswered prayer changes in the comfort of a warm blanket hug. All I had to say was, "I'm cold," and someone would fetch me another warm blanket!

My brave new world was like a darkened theater, an intensive care unit, where joy or tragedy unfolded before unwilling audiences amid sights, sounds, smells and senses which assault every area of peace for both patient and family. No one ever wants to purposely go to the hospital, and never ever wants to be a patient there, but like a novel with a surprise ending, life often has a way of taking us down unexpected paths.

Simultaneous to all the hospital drama, my experiences were vastly different. Engaged in visions, dreams, or something else, I existed in stark contrast to the bustling excitement in the ICU. I heard it said when in a coma, the neocortex ceases to function. This section of the brain is where thoughts, language and emotional elements of the personality are controlled. Upon learning the remedial details of my disconnected brain, I was perplexed. As already mentioned, it is best compared to an offline computer. The equipment is still on the ready and operational, which meant I was able to feel emotions, reason with what I saw, and recall memories of what I believe was a heavenly encounter. Although doctors are not able to explain what I went through, narrating what happened is equally puzzling. The journey to restoration was on the horizon, but the road to recovery would not be immediate. Yet to be unveiled was the most unbelievable adventure of all. For me a more than miraculous, wholly unearthly and extraordinary quest was already underway.

CHAPTER SIX

Heaven Can Wait

...I saw a vast crowd, too great to
count from every nation
and tribe and people and language,
standing in front of the throne and before the Lamb.
Revelations 7:9 (NLT)

Memories and Marvels

To reiterate, on the drive to the emergency room my heart stopped,
my lungs failed, and my airway was completely restricted. Hospital
speak said, I coded! Debates about what really happened are
ongoing. Was I dead or just near death? I cannot say for certain,
because doctors never officially pronounced me "permanently" dead.
Though I definitely experienced (as the medical dictionary defines
death) *"the cessation of all essential functions of the body including the*
heartbeat, brain activity...and breathing."[24]

In laymen's terms the best definition I can verbalize for what
transpired is when our consciousness, (the part of the brain controlling
emotion, language and thought), shuts down or no longer functions

---

[24] *http://medical-dictionary.thefreedictionary.com/death*

in the normal sense. We still experience emotions, are able to reason and process ideas, and can be fully responsive to stimuli. During near death episodes, physicians cannot explain what happens beyond the body's physical reaction. Clearly, the death of the body is not the end of the mind, nor does it mean the end of individuality. As others have reported, the human experience continues once we leave our physical body. Emblematically, I propose what I encountered was the difference between *resurrection* versus *resuscitation*. While Jesus was raised from the dead, I was merely revived.

I cannot rightly say I was literally dead. Maybe I was near death, which is defined by psychologists as *"apparently being outside the body and aware of it."*[25] Perhaps what I experienced was more of a spiritual thing, like the Apostle Paul who was "… caught up to the third heaven" *(2 Corinthians 12:2)*. "I don't know…only God knows," Paul said.[vii] Whatever the diagnosis, I was unaware anything happened to my body or that I had been in an unconscious state of **limbo** for roughly five days.

It was Dr. Hannah, anesthesiologist, who affirmed when in a *drug-induced state*, patients cannot dream! In fact, it is generally a medical impossibility since standard operation protocol dictates *administration of medication* to ensure patient has no traumatic memory or surgery recall. Basically nothing in the way of actual evidence exists to support or deny whether or not I was dreaming. However, I did experience something, although according to experts, not an ordinary dream state since my drug induced paralysis was lengthy and hindered normal dream functions.

Heavenly Introduction

After blackout and coding in what seemed instantaneous, I awoke to the sight of Cynthia Ogden. Cynthia was a doctor, a friend and partner in the ministry who died prematurely nine months prior to my

---

[25] *http://www.thefreedictionary.com/near-death+experience*

incident. Her face appeared so calm as if she had been waiting for me. As I was reclining, I looked up into her beautiful countenance. Oddly, we did not touch. If you know me, you know "I'm a hugger." However, we did not physically connect at all during my time in heaven.

"Time in heaven," sounds unreal--yet the memory of this amazing adventure is more than a dream and unlike anything I have ever encountered on earth. Heavenly thoughts still linger when alone in prayer. It may seem hard to believe, but I often cry thinking about my short visit to paradise. I miss the degree of intimacy with the Lord and want to be near Him again in the same precious way. In an effort to rationalize what doctors called "emotional instability" my experience was described by some as "just a normal reaction to a near death experience." Or another explanation for *"witnessing heaven"* could have been a natural response to replacing six of the ten pints of blood in my body. Whatever the cause, it is my prayer (by sharing these observations) the memories may inspire and even edify readers. Frankly what I experienced was more like a fantasy, many of the details are vague and meanings are cryptic. Still, there is truth to be gleaned from the things I saw. Strangely, I was unaware my body had stopped all essential functions and did not know death was imminent.

Opening my eyes to Cynthia leaning over me, I was astounded to see her without her pillow. Because of pain caused by bone cancer (which took her life after a five year battle), towards the end she carried a cushion, I assumed for comfort. Her face was radiant, clear, no spot or wrinkle. I remember thinking, "How could this be?" The response came to me, "because she is without sin," (no sin on her or in her). She was perfect the way the Lord created her to be. Overtaken by emotions, I noticed her hair was like the sun. No, it was more than that! Beams of actual sunlight were shooting out the ends of blonde locks which framed her face. She was flawlessly beautiful, nothing of the world on her. She was pure love. Her smile took my breath away. In the world Cynthia was a beautiful woman, but now she looked one-hundred times more captivating than anyone I had ever seen before. She was so graceful. All her gestures were fluid light, flowing like water; more than a dance. I found myself wondering if I should worship her.

She encompassed all the beauty of a sunset or the crystal blue ocean going on forever in a glittery wave. Unfortunately words cannot describe it any better than that, but suffice to say she now has an indescribable godly splendor. Not that she was embarrassed by my adoration, but without words she kept my response at bay. Seeing her in this renewed condition was a startling sight, because less than a year before I watched death overtake her until she finally succumbed to the disease that turned her gray, gaunt, thin and frail. At death her body was like a shell of the person she once had been, the flicker of life, the flame of the spirit gone!

I could never understand why she did not get healed because she lived as a woman of great character and faith. Truly God's ways are not our ways and His thoughts are not our thoughts *(Isaiah 55:8-9).* She was such a good person and lived humbly, in spite of a career affording her a more lavish lifestyle. She loved children, especially the Native Americans. She preferred her money to be used to bless others and help them live better lives. Funny, she was always lifting people up, now she was helping me too.

In contrast I suddenly felt the burden of my own sins; the weightiness disabled me. Like the color white, until you see it next to a more brilliant shade, you really do not understand, nor are you aware of how dirty your sins really are. *Isaiah 6:5* says, "Woe to me for I am ruined, for I am a man of unclean lips, and I live among a people of unclean lips." I felt uncovered. I stood, but I wanted to kneel. Exposed and humbled, Cynthia did not reject or denigrate me. Our connection was supernatural. I would describe it by saying "people in heaven are connected." I call it "***to be fully known***," meaning no concealing thoughts or feelings. What you see, others see too. They see in you and through your eyes, but even more, they really ***see*** you, all of you, the real you, the hidden "you" we tend to withhold from the world. Remarkably, you *perceive* them too! Basically, you know me and I know you, but in knowing each other we ebb and flow together in a unity so unearthly. Reunited with my friend Cynthia,[26] nothing was secret. Our spirits spoke to one another. As in all my encounters in heaven, we did not actually open our mouths to speak, but we knew each other's thoughts. It felt so natural!

The Rooms in My Father's House

As I looked at her she asked, "Do you want to see some rooms in my Father's house?" My reply was quick and simple, "Yes, of course." More than meager affirmation, I was thinking, "are you kidding me? Of course I want to see my Father's house." Scripture quotes Jesus speaking to his disciples, "In my Father's house are many mansions:[27] if it were not so, I would have told you. I go to prepare a place for you" *(John 14:2)*.

The Father's house has many rooms for worship, the kind of worship represented by every artistic expression, every gesture and every word or song of praise. He is all knowing, all seeing, everywhere. In an unfamiliar, anomalous way, while in heaven I felt like I was wearing Him. Like Gideon in *Judges 6:34*,[28] who is described as though God clothed him, and put His Spirit upon

---

[26] Following Cynthia's death, Matteo Guyro, a friend of both Trevor and Adina, passed away prematurely. Being so close, Adina wondered why Matteo, a young man in his thirties, did not greet her in heaven instead of Cynthia. Perhaps, greeting people as they cross into the afterlife is a reward given to very special people. Maybe we will all have some heavenly task, an important role disclosed when we enter the pearly gates. There is so much we do not know and must accept by faith regarding the afterlife.

[27] In the NIV version of *John 14:2*, the scripture says, "My Father's house has many rooms…."

[28] For more information on this subject see English Standard Version or Young's Literal Translation for specific references to being "clothed by the Spirit."

Gideon like a glove, He is also in you, through you, and all around you. I never saw God face to face, but I knew Him and He knew me. He embraced me with His presence and invited me to enjoy this heavenly place. Worship was the only proper response. Cynthia was my chaperon guiding me through this amazing heavenly community, and she did so while humbly supporting and observing. Instantly, we entered the first of many rooms I passed through. This chamber contained people worshipping in an unfamiliar language, but as I participated in what can only be compared to affectionate prayer, my understanding flourished. I went into many rooms with many languages and many different kinds of people. Present, every tribe and tongue all singing worship to the Lord.

Movement is instantaneous and so different from what we experience in our physical body. There is an overwhelming sense of "*knowing,*" a feeling of completeness without physical limitations. The Bible says, we know only in part, but when we die, we gain full knowledge, "For now we see in a mirror dimly, but then face to face. Now I know in part; then I shall know fully, even as I have been fully known" *(1 Corinthians 3:12, ESV).* In a manner of speaking, I glimpsed what I can only call *eternity*!

Surprisingly, there was no language I did not understand. Entering each room, I joined the worship in progress. The people offered up reverential praise with intense joy all for God's glory. The adoration engulfed me as I gave reverence to the King of kings and the Lord of lords. There was no music, per se. The sound of harmonious praise came from the voices, which sounded like the harp, the flute, and the trombone. All instrumental sounds were represented. Everything, the resonance, the music and the melody flowed from out of their bodies as worship. And there were different songs of adulation too. They were not tunes I knew or had ever heard before...each composition performed a new song! Heaven's music is the most beautiful sound, the singing and each tone made by a person creating their own magnificent love sonnet, which became a part of a loftier ballad where instruments were unnecessary. There was a grander richness woven together like a tapestry of musical veneration. I brought something new to the sound, an added instrument, which had lyrics expressing my love to His loveliness. The chorus chanted the facts, which heaven cannot deny, "He is holy. He is good." The worship was not just something I heard; my spirit heard it too. The songs spoke of who He is. I had no idea how long I had been in worship, whether an hour or many years, there were no clocks or concept of time.

Wondering how I understood every language, I remember saying, "Right now, I am the smartest person on the planet. I speak thousands of languages." I was so sure when I returned home, I would remember them and be able to communicate in this way the rest of my days. Well, of course I do not, but for a brief moment, I felt pretty clever. Cynthia was tickled. I knew she was amused at my expense, but I did not care. Clueless of the length of time in worship, emotions overwhelmed me until I nearly felt like exploding. Exultation to the Lord caused a tremor throughout my body as words of love were offered like gifts to the Father. The voices sang, "We know He is good. We know He is great." But in heaven you really do **know** it. There are no doubts, no fears, no confusion—you do not question the truth of His existence. The very reality of this fact is emphatically known.

In that treasured moment, I knew for certain if God were to take his hand off the world, everyone would feel it, even those who deny He exists. Atheists would feel the shift in the very structure of the universe. I sensed God knows all. He cares about everyone and every tiny detail of our lives just as scripture says He does.[viii]

While learning the purpose of every room was worship, I continued on my tour with Cynthia, whose ability to worship far surpassed my own. As well, all rooms were provisional, meaning everything was supplied. Whatever you were lacking, whatever your need, you instantly had the skills and materials at your disposal. In heaven you have every gift needed to master any artistic endeavor. "Every good and perfect gift is from above, coming down from the Father of the heavenly lights who does not change like shifting shadows" *(James1:17 NIV)*.

"It's true! I could dance." I was like a part of the Alvin Ailey Dance Troupe, jumping like a gazelle with my legs gracefully soaring effortlessly into a grand jeté caught mid-air. No one was a spectator, everyone danced their own ballet. There is something about dance that moves me to tears. Dancing is an opportunity to experience freedom like at no other time; nothing held back, no chains or constraints. A detonation of energy that tingles your toes and gestates into a massive exhale as you articulate every fiber of joy from the tips of your fingers to the top of your head resonating down to your feet. I was compelled to dance because of my love for Him. You feel the love and must express yourself in every creative form. I danced because I was overcome—I felt like I had wings and I could express my love for the Lord by dancing, so I did. What I hungered for in life, I experienced in heaven!

In another room, everyone could create and construct anything like paintings or sculpture. If you wanted to paint landscapes or portraitures like the work of Leonardo Da Vinci, you could. The talent is available to us all—everything is available. From an assortment of stone-like objects, I picked up what seemed like a rock, but felt and moved like chalk in my hand and began to draw an expression of my love for Jesus, a beautiful landscape with colorful flowers. I was amazed. Drawing talent, no problem! How did I become all things as the word says in *Philippians 4:13,* "I can do all things through Christ which strengthens me" *(KJV).*

We worshipped through song, dance, art, even the spoken word. There was a room where people could convey their **words** as a form of worship. The Bible says, man speaks out of what is in his heart[ix], and this truth is even more real in heaven, because you are speaking out of what encircles you. Surrounded by a spirit of love, the power of all

His attributes rushed through me and became a part of my essence.[29] I experienced a river flowing from within, just like the old hymn says:

> There is a river that flows from deep within.
> There is a fountain that frees the soul from sin.
> Come to the water; there is a vast supply.
> There is a river that never shall run dry.
> Lyrics by Jimmy Swaggart, 1972

In this room, I worshipped through the ***spoken*** word: "You are my Healer, my Strong Tower," all sorts of expressions of love to Him and for Him gushed out of my soul, redirected inward toward the place in my heart where the Father dwelt. The meaning was pressed home, we cannot go by what we think or what we see, but rather by what is the truth about God. Words can be restrictive and this manuscript's message is limited as I lack terms to articulate. It is hard for me to express something so humungous, but on earth that is all we have. In heaven we will communicate with words we do not speak now.

Words come out of your mouth—a spoken word—each filled with every eloquent earthly expression of adoration and more:

> How do I love thee? Let me count the ways.
> I love thee to the depth and breadth and height
> My soul can reach.
> - Elizabeth Barrett Browning
(*Sonnets from the Portuguese*, 1850)

Jesus said, "… for out of the abundance of the heart his mouth speaks" *(Luke 6:45, ESV)*. The beauty of the written and spoken

---

[29] Meaning: "the basic nature of a thing: the quality or qualities that make a thing what it is, the special qualities of the thing from which it is taken." Source, Merriam-Webster Online Dictionary: *http://www.merriam-webster. com/dictionary/essence.*

word will be experienced in a deeper and more profound way for those who enter heaven. There in the presence of the Lord, I really began to understand what this verse tries to teach about the **living Word**. Like poetry, words try to express how you feel about the Lord. Concepts and words I was never able to voice became available.

We casually use the word "awesome" to describe something we think is incredible, but until you see heaven, you cannot possibly know what **awesome** really means. I want to go back so I can learn the fuller meaning. When you go to heaven, the experience, the splendor is so much bigger than we are. My body, dressed only in my flesh suit, could not take what was happening. It felt as if my spirit was trying to rise up and break out…music was speaking to me and my body was overwhelmed by what my spirit was yielding to. Today it takes a lot out of me to tell the story. Mere words are just not adequate. The best part though is I know we are changed in His presence. This experience left His mark on me!

Faith was another separate building (though not like what we think of a structure with four walls), nor was the room connected to the main house. Tangible places existed for other words like peace, love, joy and the other remaining fruits of the spirit. Although I only visited and experienced faith, I understood spiritual fruits are more than meager words. "Faith" conveys concepts of righteousness only fully realized in Christ. During this encounter, it almost seemed like the "word" became flesh. I best liken it to Jesus strolling on the water and inviting Peter to step out of the boat in *Matthew 14:24-31*. Peter asked Jesus to beckon him to join the miraculous event on the surface of the Galilean Sea. This disciple stood and in faith, stepped onto the surface of the water. Peter may have stepped on water, but he stood on faith.

In hindsight with this image as my guide, I understood while stepping into the entrance, *Faith* is actually a quantifiable location. When standing in the midst of Faith (a belief based on trust and hope), the meaning of the word becomes obsolete. Faith lives in you;

you are in faith and it surrounds you. You touch Faith, as if it is a living, breathing word, and in heaven, it is! Words become tangible, real, more physical than anything in earthly form creating in a sense a new dimension.

Everyone in heaven was clothed in the Spirit of the Lord who engulfed each person, covering them with His glorious light. It was as if they wore Him as a robe of righteousness.[x] I was not clothed as they were, but I wanted to be. My nakedness was very apparent both physically and spiritually, it is a vulnerability that goes deeper than flesh. I could have been wearing a ten piece ensemble, but would still have been naked. There are so many different ways to worship the Lord. There were many more rooms I did not go into, but I knew they were all for the purpose of personal worship and breathtaking communion with our God. I worshipped with the people, but I could not handle it. Their breath and song to Him encompassed such passionate fire. I tried to emulate the same and grew more fatigued.

I was so exhausted! I felt my body could not sustain any more worship. I was spent expressing love and adoration *to and for* the King. It brought me to my knees spiritually. I was worshipping with the people, but could not handle the passionate overload. In my zeal, I became aware this spiritual devotion could not be contained within the mortal body. I was teeming with emotion and felt as though I would explode into a thousand little particles, each declaring a new found ecstasy for loving God. I am not sure how I moved away from the worship rooms, but as already stated, when I did I felt totally drained.

All I could think was, "Heaven is the real deal!"

Streets of Gold

People want to know and are always asking questions like "what does heaven look like?" What I recall is you are in many places at once and the space you are in is not ordinary walls with colors, paintings or furniture. Material things are there, but in God's presence they do not grab your attention, nor do you focus on their absence, because the real beauty and color of heaven is the presence of the Lord. He is everywhere in everything. I believe the reason I have such a hard time with pictures in my mind of heaven or things like angels, clouds and all the other associated clichés' is because when you are there, you do not see the presence of the physical, but rather you feel it in dimensions too numerous and wonderful to describe. Perhaps my mind, limited by critical or cognitive skills, could barely hold such miraculous imagery. Even now telling this story causes a sort of grief---it is weird. I want to be there! I do not want to die, but I cannot help the feeling that drives me and my desire to be home in my Father's house. Now, I feel like an alien, a true pilgrim in this world, someone just passing through to another life.

> I remember plopping down from exhaustion. I had to rest for a minute. As I was sitting there, I looked around, and happened to glance down from the curb where I was perched, "Hmm, streets of gold," I thought. I have never held a gold bar in my hand, but the street surface looked like gold bricks. I took my finger and scratched one, but it did not yield. I remember thinking "Is this gold?" Cynthia standing nearby began to laugh.
>
> I looked at her, and she asked, "Don't you read your Bible?"
>
> "Yeah, of course," I thought. My friend was laughing at me, but I was still in awe. Heavenly streets really are paved in gold![30]

---

[30] *Revelation 21:21:* "And the street of the city was pure gold, like transparent glass."

Then I asked her, "Why am I so tired?"

And she responded, "Because you are still in your earthly body."

I knew I did not have a spiritual body yet, nor did I have a glorified one.[xi] Nevertheless, I never thought about death. I knew I was still in my body, but also that I was not on earth. I noticed everyone in heaven had what I would describe as an absolutely glorious physique. With a god-breathed spirit removed of sinful, mortal flesh, their human form remained recognizable, but their heavenly spirits were renewed.[xii] My spirit, however, was still somehow anchored to earth.

After touring many of the rooms in my Father's house, it occurred to me, I never saw Him, nor did I witness any heavenly angels. Still, the presence of the Lord was so tangible. I did not see Him, but he was everywhere. He was always with me--touching my soul! As we moved away from the Father's house, I could hear voices giggling and playing.

"I can hear the children. Where are the children?" I asked Cynthia.

"They are near the throne. They are with the Father," she said.

In that moment it occurred to me how much the Father loves children,[xiii] so much so He wants them to be near, playing at His feet where he can delight in them. He loves them so much, He instructs us to be more like them. In the world, children are ordered to be seen and not heard. They are often last, but in heaven, they are first! With a childlike excitement, I wanted to join the laughter and be part of the revelry.

"I want to see Him. I want to go."

And she replied, "You can't see the Father because it's not your time."[xiv]

I remember feeling upset. I thought, "What!" I really wanted to see Him. I did not care about going back to my former life or anything else at that precise moment. I just wanted to be there with Him.

The High Place

Cynthia tried to comfort me with her smiles. Her expression was kindness — again she shared with me the "*knowing*." I saw it in her eyes. Suddenly I felt a strong presence. My Lord was attentive to me and understood my need to be near Him. He let me know He is always truly aware of each individual. The Lord is conscious of what we want and need. Sometimes we feel alone, but know God is sensitive to every detail of your life, and is always with you.[xv]

His word to us is, "I am mindful... I see you. I know the desires of your heart. I see *you*." And again He says, "I really see **YOU!**"

There is a depth of passion, of trust, a feeling of acceptance, but it is more than that. Simply put, He loves us. He gets it. He feels it too. His greatest desire is for you to see Him also, because He is watchful and thoughtful. And the more I wanted to see Him, the more I felt His presence.

Soon I was instantly caught up in this high place, even higher than before, but I did not know where I was. I could see myself floating above everyone else below. I was looking down past my own feet. The Lord was behind me lifting me higher and higher. Like an elevator moving me up, but the sensation was one of "heaviness," although I was at peace. I trusted the Lord. Since I am afraid of heights, this was a real odd spectacle, yet my spirit was responsive,

"I will go wherever you take me, Lord." I do not mean to make this a huge theological debate. I can only report what I remember and explain what it meant to me.

It is so funny because, as already stated, I never saw the Lord, but I knew His presence was with me like a living shadow. Think of Peter Pan's lively silhouette—who stepped off the original. Perhaps an *energy* is what the third-person of the Trinity is like;[31] a corporeal figure adhering to God and everyone else. But not like a fickle, *shifting shadow* as noted in the Book of James.[32] The Spirit is constant and consigned[33] with the fragrance of god-ship, unlike shadows, meaning darkness or obscurity, but rather a reflected image (like a breath on a mirror), an essence of something so much more that is invisible to the eye, but perceptible and real. As for the Trinity, I knew the Father was on the throne and Jesus at His right hand, so by process of elimination, I must have been dealing with the Holy Spirit, the presence, power and breath of God,[xvi] which He gave to mankind at creation.[34] Shadow is how I would describe this manifestation. The Spirit is definitely tangible and because He lives in us (the energy—the life source), we are all made one with the Lord.

The Holy Spirit is every bit as real as the other parts of the Trinity. I believe God's presence in us is the Holy Spirit, the Helper, the Counselor, the Advocate, the Intercessor walking among us. Jesus said, "…I tell you the truth: it is to your advantage that I go

---

[31] The Holy Spirit is described in the Old Testament as energy, *Zechariah 4:6*, "Not by might nor by power, but by My Spirit,' says the Lord of hosts" *(NKJV)*.

[32] See *James 1:17*.

[33] Meaning committed.

[34] *Genesis 2:7:* "Then the Lord God formed the man of dust from the ground and breathed into his nostrils the breath of life, and the man became a living creature" *(ESV)*.

away, for if I do not go away, the Helper will not come to you. But if I go, I will send him to you" *(John 16:7, ESV)*. My mindset now is whether in heaven or on earth, I make every effort to always remember the Father, Son and the Holy Spirit are One.[35]

During this very personal time, He pointed out the people below us. I noticed they were in prayer. In fact, I could feel people praying for me. I could hear the people, saying, "Adina, Adina." They were calling, but I felt restless. I did not want them summoning me. Although I felt safe, I knew if I fell forward or back I would be cushioned by their prayers. Dr. Cynthia was always there but never stood in front where I could see her. When the Lord engaged my attention, His essence was always in the forefront, because God's *presence* (in whatever form) always gets the glory. I kept looking down and saw the church, Grace to the Nations, and her people. Pouring out the doors and windows of the building were gold threads that spread all over Tucson, and they multiplied and grew towards Phoenix, then they spread to Texas and beyond.

What is that?" I asked the Holy Spirit.

"It's prayer!"

I could see the gold thread woven like a tapestry, every thread seemingly going through every home into every city, then into the county, the state, the nation and into the world.

Then the Lord said, "That's prayer for you!" I could not grasp the concept.

---

[35] *1 John 5:7:* "For there are three that bear record in heaven, the Father, the Word, and the Holy Ghost: and these three are one" *(KJV)*.

> I thought, "I don't even know this many people."
> Although I did not speak, He responded, "Yes, but
> "**I**" do!"

All I could do was watch this glowing shimmering liquid thread of prayer spilling out of the church, bending and twisting as it covered the earth. I was impressed because it moved like lava, a fluid *gold* strand. I was also taken aback that prayers, like gold, are so valuable to the Lord, incorruptible, opulent and highly malleable. Revelation captivated my imagination as the words came to me: "Our prayers are like gold to the Father." What a profound truth and precious gift. I was so blessed at the unexpected prayers that so many would lift my name.

When I saw the prayer for me all I could ask is, "Why?" I was undone by the abundance and the extravagance of His love for me and the expression of His people. He did not respond, but rather let me absorb the idea as I attempted to take in an experience so much bigger than me. I still cannot handle the blessing. I do not feel worthy, "so undeserving." But know this beloved, God's blessings and love are not about what we deserve. His work in our lives is to emphasize His goodness and unfailing love. The blessings are merely another expression of who He is. There is so much more I saw that cannot be communicated. I appreciate the Apostle John's words, "Now there are also many other things that Jesus did. Were every one of them to be written, I suppose that the world itself could not contain the books that would be written" *John 21:25 (ESV)*.

Departure

Desperation over took me. I wanted to see God, I wanted more, more of His love, more of His presence, MORE. But Cynthia was telling me I had to go. To depart meant separation. Sadness pressed my soul. "You are not going to be able to stay," Cynthia said. She knew this message was going to break my heart. Though she was gentle about it and so kind, like a physician using her best bedside manner, filled with compassionate sorrow, she knew this refusal would hurt. I felt frustrated and this is hard to say, because even though I wanted to stay, the Lord wanted me to return to my life. It was the will of God! And like our Lord in the Garden of Gethsemane, I know the correct response is always, "Your will be done, Lord!"[36]

The details of what happened next were utterly confusing, but will be developed later in the book. For now, I was returning to my body and awaking in the hospital. Contrasting where I had been in the presence of the Lord, transferring to my earthly body became terrifying and perplexing. In what felt like mere moments, I experienced the polar opposite of joy unspeakable. In heaven I had freedom, unlimited movement, love, understanding and peace. Dissimilarly, on earth I was tied down in every way possible, both physically and emotionally. All the medical equipment had me bound to a hospital bed. I was unable to speak and barely able to see the surroundings in the room, nor could I relate to my situation. How did I get here? Even my mind was tied up and disoriented.

My last memory, surrounded by the presence of God, ended abruptly. I woke and remember thinking I went from heaven straight to hell.

---

[36] Matthew 26:42

CHAPTER SEVEN

Hell In A Handbasket

The cords of hell were round me: the
nets of death came on me.
Psalms 18:5 (BBE)

Deployed from heavenly light, I awoke to a dimly lit space, crowded with people going in and out of what seemed like a murky void. Overly excited movement disguised their peculiar appearance hiding thoughts behind grotesque alien-like masks. Their flesh was merely a spacesuit façade made of a thick epidermis. All ICU visitors were covered with pale yellow gowns and electric blue gloves shielding their eerie exterior. These swirling notions confused me, creating a sense of trepidation. Anxiety and dread were enhanced by the rapid robotic and rhythmic movements of many strangers. It was surreal, slow motion in fast forward speed. I felt saturated in isolation.

Rude Awakening

My first recollection was the beeping noises that never stop in an infirmary. The breathing machine put out sounds of air pressed through a reversed vacuum; the heart beat monitor was beeping too. The phone was always ringing, calls about me, but the hospital would not give out information to anyone except family. The machines dialogued among themselves and the noise was distracting. The non-stop clamor is the hardest part of hospital care. I could not rest, yet part of me was afraid to close my eyes. I did not want to fall asleep for fear I would wake up in yet an even more bizarre world. The nurses talked in the hallways, doctors instructing them; whispers and plots, no doubt. I lost track of time and had no clue whether it was night or day.

I could not believe God sent me to hell! Truly, that is what I thought when I first opened my eyes. I was undone, so upset. "Why would You do this? What did I do?" I still felt connected and was tapped into the Lord through my spirit,[37] but unable to use my mouth. My lively thought processes pondered why He sent me to a place of torture.

Vision, reason, and interpretation of what I saw were, no doubt, influenced by morphine. But at that precise moment it was my reality. I felt every terrifying moment of powerlessness and fear brought on by confusion about where I was and how I got there. As previously mentioned, I have no memory of the week before the incident. My last tangible thoughts were of a friend's daughter Kendra B, who spent the night with me on her birthday January 29th. Then I awoke in what I thought, for a day or two, was actually hell. Though exile lasted only two days, I felt abandoned by the Lord. Like the rich man who begs for Lazarus to dip his finger in some cool water to douse his burning tongue *(Luke 16:24)*, I was in a sepulcher awaiting rescue.

The ICU's chaotic venue housed lots of different people, but

---

[37] Theological side note: We all share in the essence of God our creator, but being connected to Him is why Jesus died following man's *Fall* as recorded in *Genesis 3:4-7*. Jesus prayed in *John 17:20-23* for the regenerative work of the Holy Spirit to "make them one, just as We are one" referring to unification of His disciples. Mankind was originally made for fellowship with God. But due to sin we are born separated from His Spirit. Because of Jesus' death on the cross, we are restored to relationship once we accept His free offer of salvation.

no one seemed human. The indistinguishable crowd did not allow me to identify or relate to anyone. The pastor was there, Trevor and family were there. Not quite human, people resembled themselves, yet materialized more like rubber, motorized likenesses. I made no eye contact with doctors and nurses. Even seeing Trevor was fear-provoking. I wanted to get away, run, but could not move. I was tied down with the respirator and breathing tube inserted down my throat, a catheter, feeding tubes, heart monitors, pain medications and antibiotics being dispersed through too many intravenous tubes and rubber hoses.

Difficult to understand what happened; for that moment, God let me feel the inability to connect with the spirit of others, (as "when deep calls unto deep," *Psalms 42:7*). During my heavenly encounter, I appreciated hearts and souls reflected like mirrors where true identity was not obscured. In heaven I could see and know everyone for who they really are, but the power to do so was gone! After returning to earth's daily grind, I learned people wear more than clothes; they don falsehoods like armor. I no longer could see people with the ***knowing,*** but everyone around me looked fake, plastic, and almost inhuman. I kept trying to tap back into the Father as I did in heaven. The presence of God that led me everywhere, felt far from me. I could not communicate with Him, so I began to cry, "Why are you so far from me Father?"

There was no response to my question, just emptiness, a hellish place, the absolute definition of hell, *somewhere without God who is LOVE!* I could feel the weight of His absence as if He left me there for a moment. I felt betrayed. The weight of my question hung in the air, "Where are you? Where am I? Lord, why would you put me here?" I believe Jesus felt despair in the Garden of Gethsemane and on the Cross at Golgotha when he said (paraphrased), "...don't take your Spirit from me, please don't turn from me Lord, and don't leave me in this place" *(Psalms 22:1* and *Matthew 27:46)*. I do not intend to remotely suggest my suffering was the same as Jesus, but I feel I got a glimpse of what He must have experienced. Menacing, at that moment, was the threat I would not again see heaven and feel *the knowing*. It was almost too much to bear.

Hope

Since I suspected strangers were pretending to be the people I know, I did not trust them, even though they smiled at me. Not until Pastor Saby Adino, a member of GTTN staff and co-laborer who formerly oversaw children's ministries, visited with her young son Emmanuel, did the oppression of **hell** break. As he entered the room, the glow of light illuminating his silhouette caught my attention. He represented a type of **purity**, an earmark of God's presence. Fear which had overtaken me, soon left. When Emmanuel smiled I knew him and saw a glimpse of the Lord fill the room. A luminous fragrance, a wind from heaven, came rushing in and hovered over him. I felt the peace of God and later realized "Immanuel"[38] means *God with us.*[xvii] I cried because I understood God did not forsake me. To prove it, He sent a messenger to remind me of His loving care.

"Hi, Miss Adina," Emmanuel smiled.

It was then that everything clicked-on for me. Emmanuel brought it with him and I heard the Lord speak, "It's okay. You're in the world."

The Lord put my right mind back in my head. Later Clarissa, whose name means brilliance, another young daughter of a friend, came in and I saw the same spirit alive in her. I said, "Thank you, Jesus." I know God is here….if for no other reason, than for the precious children, the pure, the untainted…the simple, whose spirits are the best examples for this world *(Matthew 18:3)*. It was such a

---

[38] Various scripture versions spell the name "Immanuel" or "Emmanuel." Either spelling is acceptable.

relief to be near them. Claire, my daughter, also brought it home, "I was on earth." Claire was wearing a similar but smaller resonance of this childlike aura[39]....a memory, a marker, of G_d[40] seemed to rest on her too.

In the moments God's essence floated over the children, I knew everything would work out for the best.[xviii] I would talk to myself, saying things like, "You're going to be okay. It's okay. Everything is going to be alright." My nieces were there, and Claire came every day. The more I saw them, assurances everything would be fine followed. I comforted myself by recalling the Word:

> I would have lost heart, unless I had believed that I
> would see the goodness of the Lord, in the land of
> the living *(Psalms 27:13 NKJV)*.

Within days, I was asking for a means to write, since the intubation tube made it impossible for me to speak. One of the first things I wrote on a notebook was, "I heard people calling my name." In fact, I was disturbed by the pull of what I will call **earthly things**. I remember thinking, "What a bother!"

Soon Dr. Robert D was told I was awake and cognizant. He could not fathom the possibility and had to see for himself. He walked into the room. This was, of course, the first time I actually met the man. Tall and slender, graying at the temples, very friendly with a kindness that put me at ease, he seemed concerned about

---

[39] The term used here for **"aura"** means "subtly pervasive quality or atmosphere seen as emanating from a person, place, or thing" per the online dictionary: *http://dictionary.reference.com/browse/aura?s=t;* and it is not to be confused with the term which refers to **auras** as they relate to the occult.

[40] *"G_d"* is a Hebrew reference to God's name, and is used here in honor of my daughter's Hebrew heritage. The "o" is intentionally left out as the Hebrew people believed God is so holy that for humanity to utter the name would make profane God's perfection.

my welfare. He wore a crisp pink oxford-styled long sleeve shirt with pearly buttons and a look of professionalism that was quite impressive. His brilliant white smile was the first thing I noticed as he lifted his hand in a formal military-styled wave. I waved back!

"Do you remember me?" he asked.

I had my paper tablet and pen, and was able to respond. [By the way, I still have all those scribbly notes in a box I keep under my bed].

"No, should I?"

He looked at me trying to determine my meaning.

"Is she confused or is she playing with me?"

Like crazy girls, Mom and my sisters blurted out hysterically, while giggling, "Oh, she's messing with ya." The hilarity in the conversation made for a light moment in so many previously dark ones. So the doctor introduced himself and denoted his involvement with my case.

I took my notebook and quickly scrawled a quirky reply. "Nice shirt. Only real men can wear pink."

He seemed disturbed at my comment or was it my humor? I honestly think he blushed - a little. So began a great patient to doctor relationship, marking a part of the lighter side of my hospital exploit. On a positive note, I was slowly returning to myself. Recovery was gradual. But first the obstacle!

Tracheal Tube Removal

A hollow breathing tube and its mechanical attachment supported my air flow. The non-stop beeping and a multitude of additional sounds merged with other technological paraphernalia: heart monitors, blood pressure displays, EKG machines, all humming in contrast to much desired silence. The commotion and the constant flow of people in and out of the care unit, not to mention continual quarter-hourly poking and prodding made the trauma of my hospital visit more frightening.

It was February 14th, and my mind was active, confused, yet thriving. I was also awake and aware something happened. I had been out of consciousness for nearly a week and could not talk because the breathing apparatus was still in place. Doctors were concerned removal of the respirator from the trachea (a large membranous tube made up of 20 robust rings of cartilage located just under the larynx), might cause deterioration of the windpipe requiring a voice box implant. With the exception of Dr. Robert, premature removal was a risky decision the medical team was reluctant to test. Due to rescue efforts, I was missing three rings of my trachea and part of the cartilage, the tube acted like a stint allowing the traumatized area of my neck to heal. Intubation for seven days would typically be enough to recover under normal circumstances, but there were a lot of uncertainties. "I had to make a decision to pull the tube and believe she would not need a tracheostomy," Dr. Robert surmised. "To wait three to four weeks to remove the trach would have added additional strain to an area already traumatized."

Two days before hospital release, doctors once again debated removal of the tracheal tube. There were actually two surgical attempts to complete the task. During the first week, Dr. Robert planned surgery, but in less than an hour rolled me back into the ICU. He spoke with Nancy.

"Why does she still have the tube?" Nancy questioned.

"Her airway was too swollen. And I am not sure if the cartilage had been cut. The tube was tightly lodged in the esophagus. So I can't pull it out," the doctor replied.

Days later he decided to try again. This time he had a medical instrument he was going to use to hold the esophagus open, but when he removed the tape and went to pull "the trach just slid right out, no problem." The doctor said he was amazed! "God is good." Nancy proclaimed.

Although nervous about the procedure, the tube was finally removed and not a moment too soon. I hated it. Taped tightly around my head and lips; immensely uncomfortable, it had a manual suction pump for removing excessive fluid from my lungs, a very painful process that made me cough. Once Trevor noticed I needed to be suctioned, and suggested another procedure be done. I adamantly refused. When he asked if I would rather get suctioned or experience pneumonia, I chose pneumonia. Struggles continued in the following days but with each enterprise, God performed miracles. The greatest of all was the prayer of faithful saints.

CHAPTER EIGHT

The Upper Room

Pray without ceasing.
1 Thessalonians 5:17, (KJV)

Prayer

Defying fatal prognoses, I started recovering due to the faithfulness of praying saints. The power of prayer goes beyond any weapon or tool utilized during endeavors with principalities working against God's kingdom or people *(Ephesians 6:12)*.[41] As I hope this testimony will establish, prayer's power was evident.

Since becoming a Christian, prayer has always been a passion of mine. For nearly two years, during the early days since I gave my life to Jesus, I spent every Monday night in prayer with other godly women from the Tucson community and beyond. I joined female pastors and several Christian leaders, anointed and powerful women to pray. These faithful warriors stood for two hours in a small circle

---

[41] *Ephesians 6:12,* "For we wrestle not against flesh and blood, but against principalities, against powers, against the rulers of the darkness of this world, against spiritual wickedness in high places."

and simultaneously prayed in the Spirit. There I learned to pray and to intercede for others.

Supplication is my way of communicating and communing with God. I have seen God move through prayer and as a result want the miraculous to continually operate in the day-to-day of all believers. Perhaps that is why so many do not join prayer groups; they do not see God moving. Prayer is merely us having an intimate conversation with Him. I speak, He listens. He speaks, I listen. For me prayer is not about what I want God to do for me, but rather to understand why He does what He does and to know Him in an intimate way. I am so in love with my God, and prayer is how we cultivate our relationship. There are times when I take my prayer request to the Lord, and other times when He just moves on my behalf by meeting a need (something I had not thought about or asked for). He shows favor for which I have no expectation. The Lord often responds with an affirmative answer, but I do not always get what I want. Still I know the Lord always gives me what I need. He is such a wonder, better than any good father. But first we have to PRAY: "...and to let your requests [prayer need] be made known to God" *(Philippians 4:6b)*.

In his book, "User Friendly Prophecy," Larry J. Randolph describes prayer in a way that speaks to me; "...prayer dials down the clamor of our soul and heightens our ability to hear and to be led by the inner witness of the Holy Spirit."[42] We often underestimate prayer's power and potential.

Prior to health crisis, we were on the last day of a twenty-one day church-wide fast for breakthroughs in relationships: families, marriages, and for our church. Some did a Daniel-like fast (just vegetables, grains, and brown rice), while several fasted the media, and others skipped meals altogether. Everyone participated in a way best suited to their individual lifestyle. I think it is no coincidence

---

[42] *User Friendly Prophecy: Guidelines for the Effective Use of Prophecy*, by Larry J. Randolph, 1998, Destiny Image, Publishers, Inc., page 32.

the world of darkness[43] chose to attack me at the end of my fast. Just like Jesus in the desert fasting for forty days *(Matthew 4:1-11)*, the enemy comes when we are at our weakest.

The Pit Crew

At that time, we had a group of prayer warriors called the Pit Crew, made up of nine ready servants who had hearts for God, prayer, and change. Trevor explains:

> The PIT crew is the Pastoral Intercessory Team, normally led by Adina to pray for Pastors Obed and Rae. Due to circumstances, Rae was leading the prayer group, with phone calls every half hour or so, with updates on Adina's status. Although encouraged to pray, they were not given a great deal of information. Rae was facilitating the prayer and until we knew something for certain we were not disclosing details. We told them, just pray because, "Right now, it is critical. She is fighting for her life."

I suppose God chose this group of leaders to ignite a prayer vigil, because they were willing and would sacrifice anything to support the leadership. The team was not necessarily considered church **elite,** but like David's Mighty Men,[44] they were dedicated to "the call," with hearts for the things of God, a desire for intimacy with the Lord, and those committed to seeking relationship with the Almighty. I counted on them to listen for the heart of God. They did not try to pray their own agenda, but stayed ready to hear the Lord's voice. Based on love for the pastors and the pastoral team, they were

---

[43] The phrase is a colloquialism referencing demonic forces or potential devilish influences.

[44] 1 Chronicles 11:10-13

immediately ready in season[xix]. *The call* meant no matter what time of day or night, they stopped what they were doing or left where they were to seek God's direction. Their hearts were devoted to the Lord while they learned skills to become seasoned spiritual warriors.

When the woman of God called,[45] "There is an emergency with Adina. I need you to go to the prayer room," the Pit Crew jumped into action. Pastor Rae sent a text to one of the Crew and it spread. Wherever they were, they came immediately to pray. Scattered all over the city at lunch, running errands, spending time with nature in the mountains, with family (it did not matter) they gathered for prayer. They dropped their plans and headed towards the *Upper Room*[46] (an affectionate reference to the prayer room at GTTN) where they all met and began to intercede.

Trevor also has his own perspective:

> To know my wife is to meet one of the most compassionate and winsome people I have ever met. She is the kind of person who approaches strangers and within five minutes they'll become best friends. I don't know how many conversations she's had that include these words, "I don't know why I'm telling you this, but..." Her congeniality opens a lot of doors and opportunities, which she takes to prayer on their behalf. Often she gives them a word from the Lord, or if needed confronts sin giving them a dose of reality. Anyone who's had a conversation with her knows exactly what I'm talking about. The Lord has used her to reach many people, and when the news of her condition spread, so did prayer.

---

[45] "The woman of God" is a pet reference used by Adina, often referring to Pastor Rae or other godly female leaders.

[46] Acts 1:13

God is calling His people to walk in the power, authority and maturity His life, death and resurrection purchased for us. Why when describing the full armor of God[47] do we leave out the part about praying all the time?[xx] God is calling us to pick up our swords of the Spirit,[48] which is the **Word of God** and engage with Him against the enemy in prayer. Not in some pious false humility, but in the knowledge and passion of who He is and what He is about. "His Kingdom come and will be done on earth as it is in heaven."[49]

Prayer Vigil

The prayer watch began in Grace to the Nations' small room above the sanctuary, and rapidly spread nationwide, even to remote areas of India, Israel, New Zealand, Peru, Brazil, Nepal, Argentina, and those are just some of the places I knew about. The prayer vigil started at roughly 5 p.m., on Monday and continued non-stop until Wednesday, 9 p.m..

Eventually the word about my health leaked to the *church elders* (spiritual leaders, shepherds of the body), and was then broadcast to Grace's general membership (aka Gracers). Everyone was praying and calling others to pray too. We are in an age of cellular technology, so the message spread like wildfire. Someone would *text a message* or *email a prayer request* and in seconds three hundred of my friends knew to pray. At the peak of prayer time, hundreds of people ushered into the fifteen by forty-six foot room. They were standing, sitting, kneeling, reading the word, praying in English, Spanish and

---

[47] *Ephesians 6:11:* "Put on the whole armor of God."

[48] Ephesians 6:17

[49] Matthew 6:10 and Luke 11:2.

Tongues[50] (an utterance gift), declaring, and prophesying, calling out to the Lord to heal and restore my life. Trevor explains:

> Tuesday night I felt a strong urge to go to the prayer room. *Gracers* had been praying every minute of every hour in that room since the incident Sunday. With pastors and the arrival of Adina's parents, sisters and brother near her bedside, I had an opportunity to step out for a couple of hours. I headed up to the prayer room and to my astonishment there were fifty plus people *standing in the gap*[xxi] for my wife.

> Some cried, others silently walked back and forth, while engaging in quiet prayer. I was blessed and humbled to see the love of the people. As I walked in, the room fell silent. I gave them a brief and general update on Adina's condition. Then, as I was speaking, the Lord led me to share some things to give them the same hope and encouragement He had given me.

> For forty-five minutes I spoke. I shared how "I was scared, but not afraid." I heard rumblings among the people regarding the fast: "How could this happen to Adina?" I felt it was allowed to happen *because* we were in a time of testing.[51] We as a church had

---

[50] *1 Corinthians 14:22,* "So you see that speaking in <u>tongues</u> is a sign, not for believers, but for unbelievers. Prophecy, however, is for the benefit of believers, not unbelievers" *(Holy Bible, New Living Translation ®, copyright © 1996, 2004 by Tyndale Charitable Trust. Used by permission of Tyndale House Publishers. All rights reserved).*

[51] Fasting can be times of testing or temptation. See Jesus's Temptation in the Desert in *Mark 1:13.*

positioned ourselves to seek God's face. It was a position that humbled us and allowed for greater access to God's grace, strength, and direction; a position that sustained us during this time of crisis.

As I conveyed this and more to the group, I could feel the mood change. The Holy Spirit was there. Where fear ruled, faith took its place. Where there was doubt or confusion, confidence and certainty captivated their imaginations. Together we knew God's will for this situation, and what to do about it. The prayer room erupted in purposeful, powerful, and confident intercession that did not simply go away when the excitement wore off, and in many ways is still going on today. I went back to the hospital encouraged, energized, and strengthened. Faith comes by hearing,[52] and as much as I was telling them what God told me, I was also encouraging myself. God is always faithful to confirm His word!

Come Forth!

During Wednesday night service instead of holding a regular Bible study, the time was used to pray collectively, both the Latino and English services met and interceded. At the end of the night, a member gifted with the prophetic spoke and said, "Just as Jesus called Lazarus[53] to come forth, we need to call Adina forth."

The house prophet stood on the pulpit and affirmed what happened to me "was not unto death."[xxii] He called those in the room

---

[52] Romans 10:7 (NKJV)

[53] John 11:43

to fill-in the spaces around the platform and began to admonish them.

> "If you have a shred of doubt or unbelief," he said, "step back."

The prayer warriors began to scream my name.

> "Adina, come forth!"

> "Adina, come forth!"

> "Adina, come forth!"

Three times they called in unison. Following their declaration, the service was over. The lengthy prayer vigil had ended. It would be four days before I would actually return to consciousness. But I definitely recall hearing someone calling my name. I remember, I stopped and felt it. Like a shout from a distance, down a dark lengthy hall, far away, but faint. "Adinaaaaaaaa...Adinaaaaaaa... Adinaaaaaa."

India Prays

Another remarkable prayer event involved my dear friend Auntie Mariamma Thampy, a mighty woman of God, whose life and ministry has touched and healed thousands, upon thousands, upon thousands worldwide, and whose life forever continues to change the face of India with her profound insight into spiritual strongholds and practical ministry. She also hosts a television program broadcasted in India that ministers the gospel through testimony and prayer. Considering the opposition she faces within India, her message for healing families living in a culture with millions of gods and so many open doors to the demonic, she is a leader of prayer ministry and an example to the world. She and her husband V. A. Thampy, founders of the ICPF (Inter-Collegiate Prayer Fellowship) and Women's Bible College, have planted hundreds of churches throughout Kerala.

During the weekend of the incident, a women's conference was simultaneously held in India. Mariamma was attending this symposium where thousands of women gathered for ministry. While at the conference she commanded the women to pray. They stopped their teaching time to lift my name before the Lord.

Worldwide Prayer

So many others have stories to share about their prayer experience. When Claudia R, twelve-year member[54] of GTTN, and I were introduced, we felt an immediate kindred spirit because of our mutual love of prayer.

We tease each other. I call her "Adina" of the Latino Church and am referred to as "Adina the Latina" by the Spanish congregation. She oversees a prayer ministry with sixty members whose mission is to evangelize our local Spanish-speaking community. She also belongs to a citywide spiritual evangelism team who are always reaching out to others with the salvation message. They never stop! For about eight years, they have gone to hospitals and supported churches throughout Tucson. They host various park events, feed the homeless, put on skits, perform puppets shows, and even visit Mexico on mission trips to minister the love of Jesus. In addition, they offer services to clean yards, clean homes, and do dishes. Whatever the need, this group provided assistance.[55]

Claudia got the news about me the same day. As a minister, she can access any hospital room and was able to get into the intensive care unit where others could not. She was visiting a friend in the room next to mine, so was able to come and go without hindrance.

---

[54] At the time of the event

[55] This group is not currently operating.

God opened a door, and only He opens doors no one can close.[56] She just walked into my room. Her shock and grief were deeply felt because, "She did not look like the Adina I know," Claudia said. Confident I could hear, Claudia spoke to me just as we always did:

> "I asked the Lord for a sign that she knew I was there. Then I saw a tear coming from the corner of her right eye." Claudia wiped it off and began singing, praying and talking to me about the Holy Spirit.

> Very moved by this tender moment, Claudia said it touched her heart. She began to pray and prophesy. She declared "The Holy Spirit is here! Do not be afraid. You will be healed, Adina." Afterwards, you could feel the presence of God in the room, Claudia said. She began to weep.

> "I felt something good was going to happen," she added. Claudia's faith that God would heal never faltered.

> "Adina, it's seven o'clock. It's time to get up," Claudia said. God's Spirit moved and left His powerful vestige on Claudia too.

Francisco and Elia Santa Cruz own Radio Vida, a Spanish radio station which airs a program every Tuesday called, "John 3:16." Francisco met me through Claudia the day of the incident, but I cannot remember the introduction. Through connections, Claudia sent out prayer requests using their prayer chain. An expressed need goes out to the public through radio waves and the praying listeners intercede 24/7. She also started calling people, who connected

---

[56] Isaiah 45:1

with others and they called even more prayer warriors. Radio Vida staff also prayed at 6:30 every morning, Monday through Sunday, requesting listeners continue praying. Claudia led these prayers on Thursdays, and different pastors led this same prayer request all the other days of the week. Lots of people prayed worldwide even over the Internet. The radio station has a globe that lights up with a red light indicating where the call for various things originated, like pray requests, praise reports, and miracles. The globe helps to visualize the location of people being touched through Radio Vida prayer. To learn more to go: *http://radiovida1210.com/web/.*

Generally, effects of praying on the radio are immeasurable, but while doing so "we felt a general assurance everything was going to be okay," Claudia said. "The whole team prayed and it felt as if everybody in the whole world was praying for Adina. I always prayed and knew the Holy Spirit was at work. We were fasting as a church. And some continued to fast and pray in the belief she would be alright."

Prayer is contagious! When we see others moved to intercede for someone it is important to remember, God is not moved by need alone. He is inspired by our *faith* (aka trust mixed with hope) and chooses to work with us to accomplish great things through prayer. "Adina has a special gift to encourage, motivate, and help me know who I am in God," Claudia said. "She always has that timely word that brings peace to any situation." How great would the *Body of Christ* be if we continued in this prayer effort all the time, lifting the needs of our brothers and sisters before the Lord?

> Now this is the confidence that we have in Him, that if we ask anything according to His will, He hears us. And if we know that He hears us, whatever we ask, we know that we have the petitions that we have asked of Him.
>
> *1 John 5:14-15, (NKJV)*

A Husband's Prayer

At times, things got pretty dark, especially for Trevor. In his own words, here is what he learned during prayer time:

> You know Lord how many people my wife has touched and how You pour Your love out to Your people through her. If You take her home, still I will serve You. If she will not be able to walk or to speak, still I will trust You. But I know You Lord. If You take her or leave her broken right now, it would hurt the faith of the people. I know the seasons we have been in, and where You are trying to take us. I know the things You have called us both to do. I cannot do it alone. In the future, if Adina operates in a greatly diminished capacity, I know You Lord, and because I know You, I pray You will heal her and raise her up in Jesus's name!

> While in prayer, I came to another realization. An allergic reaction after a conversation about God healing my wife of a peanut allergy [something Adina talked about with The Booths' in the Green Room the day of the incident], coming to the end of a church-wide fast, and the Couple's Valentine's Day weekend conference, it was clear. This was not a simple case of unfortunate events. This was not a scrape or bruise due to living in a fallen world. This was a spiritual attack at a high level. But God always held Adina in the palm of His hand.

> Given the circumstances, this event was an attempt to end Adina's life. Rather than acting out of fear or getting angry with God, this knowledge

filled me with expectation in God's promises. As I kept saying, "I was scared, but not afraid, and never without hope."[57] What the enemy meant for destruction, He will turn and use for good. *Romans 8:28* says "…all things work together for good to those who love God, and are called according to His purpose." Love for my wife grew with every prayer, every time I helped her up, every dose of medication, and every tear I wiped away. As we have been walking this out, each step has shown me more and more just how much Jesus loves *His Bride.*

What a joy learning the extent of my husband's love, and realizing friends, many relationships forged during ministry cared diligently for my welfare while passionately petitioning the throne of God for my healing. This may be hard to understand for some, but the presence of the Lord in all His love, warmth, and greatness – even in my diminished state – was so much greater than any other feeling, thought or dream. I can only stand in awe of the *power of prayer* and the influence of God's presence in our earthly pain. Only prayer can bring the support needed to bear any horrific situation. Trevor said it well, "Christians need to be a people of prayer." Hot pursuit of God means customarily communing with Him as only prayer can do.

Strangers Pray

Not only did my husband have prayer experiences, so did my daughter. Tucson Hebrew Academy (THA) had been Claire's school since 2005. A student there since first grade, with peers all ages up to eighth grade, Claire had just graduated seventh. "I know all 150

---

[57] Interpretation: Based on the meanings of these words: **scared** means sudden fear or terror; and **afraid** means filled with apprehension. Trevor's statement was a declaration of degree, while at the same time he was not without hope!

students, and am close with my 13 classmates," said Claire. "It is a private school. I am one of the only, if not *the only*, person of color." Since first joining THA, she always walked closely with members of her Jewish roots. It is a small school so everyone stayed connected. The family support has always been fervent, and something I felt really strongly during recovery. Claire shares her observations:

> "On Passport to Peace Day..." [a mandate for students to focus on improving the world where they live, while learning about cultures, tolerance and how their efforts can make a difference in the world], "we helped different organizations with various fundraisers," said Claire. "When my classmates heard about my mom, they prayed."

Praying for me to recuperate was just another example of how they were trying to make a difference, and how God used every voice to move in my favor. Anyone can become a part of changing things and prayer is the greatest weapon of choice. Prayer moves mountains![xxiii] An example of God's amazing gift of prayer bestowed on believers is as Jesus said in the *Book of Mark*:

> And these signs will follow those who believe...they will lay hands on the sick, and they will recover. *(Mark 16:17-18b, NKJV).*

In hindsight, I see how the Lord was guiding me through the drama. From the GTTN Latina women who worked in the hospital in housekeeping, to all the nurses and doctors, I had the most incredible care. It moved me to tears to learn these women specifically came into my room every night when I was totally out of it, and prayed in the Spirit over me.

Another crazy prayer moment not revealed until a year later, involved visitors to our Sunday service. Similar to a Teen Challenge group, we had members from what we lovingly called the *"X Church"* visiting Grace. Members of the church proudly declared they were ex-junkies, ex-prostitutes, ex-over eaters, and so on. Out of San Diego, they came to GTTN to minister to us through worship, the Word, testimony and song. Prior to the service, I decided to greet them at the door as they entered the sanctuary. They enthusiastically exited their chartered bus, seeming eager to begin this special time of ministry, so I introduced myself.

> "Hi, I'm Pastor Adina. Welcome to Grace to the Nations."

> One bright face shouted, "You're Adina."

> "Yes, I'm Adina."

> Turning to the women following her, she announced, "This….is Adina."

> The responses came back from her companions. "This is Adina?'

> "Yah? The one we've been praying for?"

> "Yah, this is her!"

The ladies began hugging me, offering words of love and support, while kissing my cheek and giving thanks to the Lord for His answered prayer. I stood in awe of God's amazing love. It was established! Hearing the story afterwards just confirmed once more the power of prayer and how the Lord hears all our requests.

Lessons to Learn

I was asked to report what affect this incident had on the church. A definite seed for prayer was planted which reinforced the knowledge God moves through prayer. So many Christians profess faith, but experience ordinary lives instead. We as a membership went through a remarkable event as one body, and *teamwork* best exemplifies what that looked like. God uses us…He does the work as we partner with Him through the discipline of prayer. The church as a whole needs to understand the power, authority and responsibility of every individual and their prayer life. Although threaded through the entire story, we are reminded God answers prayer even if it seems impossible, and now we can say we know how to pray for those needing healing in our circle.

The God of Abraham, Isaac, and Jacob

The prayer stories are diverse. Shortly after reviving, still in bed with a tube in my mouth, I was able to see a window right in front of me, the kind with the old school blinds, really wide and ecru, colored so by time. The blinds were closed but broken in spots with fragments missing. For whatever reason, my room was the only one with a glass window pane separating the adjacent room. All other ward rooms had solid walls. Not sure why my room was designed with a window, but God is the master chess player, putting each piece in place ready for war in His time. Through the blinds' small openings, I could see the patient across the room, a woman who my sister later told me was older and very sickly. With the exception of the doorway, she was my sole visual purview outside the space of the depressing hospital walls.

Set within my story, this dying woman's narrative revealed God's power and desire to heal. All I knew about my semi-roommate, at the time, was like me she was fighting for life. I could see her family coming in and out of the ward. One gentleman was so grieved by the drama he kept wringing his hands and running them through his hair as he paced the floor. I could feel his pain as every motion communicated as much. He displayed such helplessness. I was also helpless, unable to console him. I knew this woman's situation was serious when the nurses kept shushing my sisters and others energetically talking amongst themselves (a sign things had turned for the better regarding me).

"You guys have to be quiet cause the woman next door is actively dying and her family is really having difficulty," she paused then continued, "You need to give them space to grieve."

I felt the presence of the Lord fall on me. He spoke to me and said, "I want you to pray for her." I did not know how. I was already praying for her in my heart. I felt grieved for her and her family, but I was in a tough spot myself. I could not talk or move from my bed.

The prayers from my heart were not enough. I felt the Lord pressing me to do more. I had a breathing tube in my mouth making it impossible for me to verbalize my thoughts, with eight different tubes and a catheter connected to my body, and no physical strength. My sister Rita was there and saw me pointing at the window.

"What? What do you need?" Rita asked. "What do you want?" And so began this game of charades.

"Do you want me to shut the window?"

"Do you want the window open?"

How could I convey what I needed her to do? Just then, the gentleman who was wringing his hands went into the hallway. I pointed at him, and again at the window.

"Oh, you want to pray for him?" Rita questioned.

Shaking my head no, I pointed to the window again.

"OH, you want to pray for the woman?" Rita began to point to the patient in the adjacent room.

With a head gesture I did my best to convey my meaning, YES!

"How you gonna' do that?" She was clearly showing her uneasiness at the fact I was expecting her to do something way out of her comfort zone.

The guessing-game continued with my effort to communicate. I wanted to form a prayer chain with me as the conduit. The Lord was speaking to me and I needed to physically connect with this nameless woman. She was just another soul standing at the precipice of her journey into eternity. Beginning with me in my bed and running over to hers about thirty feet away, I wanted to form a human procession to carry the spiritual gift God had for this grief-stricken family to the vessel for whom He meant to receive it. Using my right arm I motioned with my forefinger pointing downward to form a visual: one, by one, by one. Rita, pointing to herself with an expression conveying all her doubts asked, "You want me to do that? Are you sure?" She went to the family and explained her sister, a pastor, wanted to pray for them. One of the most miraculous revelations about our broken down communication chain involved Rita's ability to understand me. This kind of unspoken communication can only happen between the truest sisters who hold each other's heart. From that point, I do not really know how it all fell into place, but Rita got on it. She gathered the people. I could hear her nervous agitation. This kind of action is so not who she is. She is the quiet one, the reserved one, so not out of the box. I just have to chuckle when I recall the look on her face. Still she was able to arrange all those in the room to form a line of people from my bed into the hallway, continuing to the patient in the next room. The nurse said, "I am not supposed to do this," as she opened the blinds so I could see. Apparently, prayer chains are not the norm at hospitals.

Rita told them, my sister wants to pray for (what I assumed was) their mother. In spite of the shock and apprehension, they permitted it. Joining the prayer chain, the nurse touched my hand and held Rita's hand, the woman's female family member held Rita's hand, another nurse held us together, then all the rest of her family prayed (about ten in all). Rita became my voice. With my left hand raised heaven-ward, I lay on my bed, but passionately interceded for a stranger. I believe my prayer, infused with the Holy Ghost, flowed through each person in the chain. Rita does not remember what she prayed, but felt it was the Lord. "I was merely a vessel of the prayer to flow through," she later recalled.

Following our group prayer, Rita walked into the room and touched the woman's foot. She told the family, "If you have faith of a mustard seed,[58] your mother will be healed." Rita said she knew that the woman did not have the faith to believe, and that they needed to believe God for a miracle. She then walked to the woman and placed her hand on her chest. Rita, familiar with the scripture, felt the Lord was speaking through her. "Although we did not pray long, I really felt like the Lord wanted to touch her and increase the faith of not just my family, but this other family too," Rita said. I remember the whole thing felt so unreal. Tears were flowing down my face. Even the nurses affirmed, "I have never **felt** anything like this before."

The next day, I noticed through my window gateway, the woman and her family were gone. My sister later shared they had moved the woman to another room, but little else was known. It was several days before the son returned to the ICU. Alone in ICU, he stopped by to see me. "I just wanted to thank you for praying for my mother," he said. He also shared with me that his mother would be returning home soon. Then he asked me a poignant question, "What God were

---

[58] Matthew 17:20

you praying to?" By this time, I had a pen and note pad, so I was able to communicate. On my pad I scribbled the words:

"The God of Abraham, the God of Isaac and the God of Jacob."

Standing as though pondering the meaning of what was said, his only response was, "Hmmm!" Looking like a man of Middle Eastern descent, I wanted him to know who my God was. I had no clue as to where he was spiritually coming from. Perhaps he believed in the god of the sun, moon and stars. No matter, I wanted to be certain he knew the name of the One I believed in, the only One worthy of worship, willing and able to heal. He looked at me, then gently touched my hand and said, "Thank you!"

Although I never doubt my God can heal and raise the dead, I assume my newly found friend was shocked by the results of our prayer chain. I later learned from ICU staff that the woman was moved to another location and returned home. Although she eventually died months later, through prayer the Lord gave her more precious time with her family before leaving this planet. Prayer is a mystery!

Polish poet Czeslaw Milosz, credited with having translated the Old Testament Psalms into Polish, wrote a poem about prayer that speaks to the mystery of what prayer can be if we seek to cultivate it by speaking our hearts, listening for His voice, and responding obediently to what He calls us to do:

> *All I know is that prayer constructs a velvety bridge*
> *And walking on it we are aloft, as on a springboard*
> *Above landscapes the color of ripe gold*
> *Transformed by the magic stopping of the sun*
> *That bridge leads to the shore of Reversal*
> *Where everything is just the opposite and the word **is***
> *Unveils a meaning we hardly envisioned.*
> *Czeslaw Milosz (1911-2004)*

Powerful Intercession

Of all the prayers that touched my heart, the words of my pastor were some of the most stirring. Pastor Rae, my mentor, my mother, my sister and my friend has become one of my most treasured relationships. Her undying love and support for me and my family will always bond us together. She shares her testimony and here in her own words, descriing her prayer experience:

> Long before our friendship began, I prayed for the Lord to bring me an assistant in the ministry. After I laid hands on Adina to receive the Holy Spirit[xxiv] with the evidence of speaking in tongues,[59] it was about a month later she inquired about a mentor relationship.
>
> "The Lord wants me to be **under** you," Adina stated.
>
> "What does that mean?" I asked.
>
> "I don't know," said Adina. "That is just what I heard."
>
> "Well, let me pray about it."

Some time passed and the pastor asked me if I was familiar with

---

[59] Jesus speaking in *Mark 16:17-18* says, "And these signs will follow those who believe: In My name they will cast out demons; they will speak with new tongues they will take up serpents; and if they drink anything deadly, it will by no means hurt them; they will lay hands on the sick, and they will recover" *(NKJV)*. If interested also see *Acts 10:45-46* in *NIV* or *NKJV*; and *1 Corinthians 14:39* in *NIV* to become familiar with more scripture references regarding speaking in tongues.

the story of Elijah and Elisha.[60] I told her "no," and she instructed me to go read about it and get back with her. Shortly thereafter I again asked Rae to mentor me, but she tried to talk me out of it:

> I don't think this is what you want to do. It does not mean sitting in my office once a week. Mentoring involves service and sacrifice. You would have to follow me, work alongside me as I am fulfilling God's call. You would have to run errands, file papers, pick up the laundry. You'll work hard." To her that was a dare. My words were a challenge she would take up with passion and a full commitment because that is her nature. Long before she was married, she came to my house for two years every day immediately after she got off work. She made herself invaluable.

> While sitting in the ER waiting room I realized, I can't live without this woman in my life. She has drilled herself into my very being and I just don't want to lose her. I began to pray. "Lord, You have to fully restore her 'cause I have to hear her laugh and listen to her wit. She knows I am her pastor and her boss. I am a spiritual mother to her in both practical and the things of God. I showed her how to dress, how to clean her house, and how to set a table. She is my right hand, and a powerful minister to the church, and so essential to all we are at GTTN. But she is more than that. She is a confidant to me and knows things nobody else knows, just as I know things about her. She has this ability to keep all the pieces of who we are right and at the right moment.

---

[60] Read more in the book of *1 Kings 19:19–2 Kings 2:15*.

I do not know how she became so woven in my life, but we are entwined. To say we are close does not fully convey all that she is to me. She has moved into the role of girlfriend, sister, comrade, cohort, compatriot in crime. She is all that and more and I am so glad and truly grateful for her life.

There is a favorite scripture found in *1 Samuel 18* verse *1,* which speaks of the friendship between Jonathan and David. This text depicts more than mere companionship, but illustrates a soul tie that knits their hearts together forever in a close bond. I like to think it explains the special relationship I share with Rae:

> Now after David's talk with Saul was ended, the soul of Jonathan was joined with the soul of David, and David became as dear to him as his very life *(1 Samuel 18:1, BBE).*

Prayer really does make all the difference in relationships, ministry, the world, life events and especially in the realization of miracles. Pastor Rae explains the power of prayer:

> The Lord uses prayer to enact His will by allowing us to become His voice. Many times we don't understand the importance of being "His Voice and Body" on earth. Doing so involves implementation of God's will, and we are left waiting for Him to respond. But we are His body here on earth; we are His voice. And nothing happens without His voice and His spoken Word. For instance, creation happened because God spoke first. In Old Testament times, God used a prophet or leader's voice to precede

the miraculous. Moses and Elijah had to articulate God's will prior to any miraculous intervention.

Jesus Christ embodied the Word of God and when He spoke, things happened. We are His body, but He is waiting for us to "become the body," which means to "be the voice." So God's work is done when we His body, His Church, in prayer articulate His will. That is why Jesus told His disciples to pray, "Your will be done on earth as it is in heaven!"[61] Jesus gave us a prayer format to voice God's will, His provision, His forgiveness and His Kingdom expansion!

As I was praying over Adina, the scripture that came to me was from Acts 12:1-11. The account details how Peter was chained in the bottom of a jail cell, shackled and doomed to die. The situation was dire because the Apostle James had just been beheaded! Now Peter, in the same situation, witnessed the church's fervent prayer. While they were speaking out scripture says – not thinking about it or begging God - the angel came and released Peter from his chains while leading him out of the dungeon. Revelation came to my heart at this moment, and I decided to stop just thinking about Adina's situation, crying over it or begging... but instead I raised my voice and proclaimed the Will and Word of the Lord over it!

We as the church must stop begging in prayer and simply verbalize our needs to God. It is time for the Church to become the voice of God on earth and start speaking His Word, His Will and His

---

[61] *Matthew 6:10* and *Luke 11:2.*

creative power in faith over the situations we face! I began to pray differently than ever before. It wasn't a pleading prayer. It was a command, an activation of the will of God. It came out of my lungs and through my natural breath. But my breath, coupled with the breath of the Holy Spirit across my vocal chords, began to voice God's own will and released His creative healing power over Adina!

"You shall live and not die in your flesh! Adina, you shall not die, in the name of Jesus. Again I say, you shall live and not die."

Trevor also heard the Lord speaking and learned a few things he wanted to share:

Almost before Dr. Robert D completed efforts to return Adina to a normal life, the Lord started speaking to my heart. "God was up to something and we were right smack dab in the middle of it!" I comforted myself with His word:

> The LORD is close to the brokenhearted and saves those who are crushed in spirit.
> *Psalms 34:18, (NIV)*

I also had peace because God spoke and said, "What has happened to your wife is a picture of my bride."

Immediately I knew what He meant. The church as a whole has allowed her breath to slowly diminish. We shorten or shirk altogether our times of prayer and getting into the Word, thereby cutting ourselves off from the very breath and Spirit of God. Then when an attack comes, we do not have the resources to endure the stress and excitement of the **enemy of our soul** and we breakdown.

God spoke to me. He said, "Once again I am going to shake heaven and earth, and My people are not ready."

He is calling His people back to a place of intimacy with Him. We are called to be in His word daily and also to pursue prayer, while being continually filled with His Spirit. His breath and words bring order, hope, salvation, and grace to a lost, sick and dying world. But, first we need our breath established in Him.

> And the Lord God formed man of the dust of the ground, and breathed into his nostrils the breath of life; and man became a living soul.
> *Genesis 2:7, (KJV)*

He Set My Feet on High Places

Finally there was my prayer. My thoughts, though oftentimes capricious, expressed desire for survival through the emotional highs and lows. I felt cut in half, not complete, like my body's nucleus was removed leaving a hole where my soul had been taken out. Occurring at the drop of a hat, revelation of where I had been caused me to burst into tears at the mere hint of a paradise moment. This sentimental onslaught was worse than the anaphylaxis which shut down my airway. I was petrified, robbed, grieving the death of a dream. Remembering random terrifying moments, I could not understand why I suffered. I felt abandoned. Of course, God's peace and logic would soon rule again as faith and trust in God's goodness returned. But the further away from my heavenly experience, the more I worried I would never again remember what I saw and felt in God's perfect domain.

Plausibly my experience is best described as *struggling with letting go* and trying to accept my fate. I was back in my body, on earth, with things to do for the Lord. Nevertheless, I wanted to be with God and could not understand why, what felt like punishment, was God's good thing for my life. What else can one do in a spot like this except to seek His face *(Psalms 105:4)*. I could not walk properly, and could not walk at all on my own, but I was determined. I grabbed my walker and began a lengthy two-step shuffle to the prayer room. At the time of my hospital release, I lived on church property, so I knew I could get there on my own. But the prayer room might as well have been one hundred miles away. The entrance was two flights of stairs above my head. Sluggishly, I began my trek to the base of the stairs that led to the *Upper Room*.

> He makes my feet like the feet of deer, and sets me
> on my high places.
>
> *2 Samuel 22:34, (NKJV)*

The winding stairwell loomed dauntingly above my head. But if I wanted to seek the Lord, I had to be in the highest place, closest to heaven, to be nearest to where His Spirit dwells. So I mounted the steps, one by one, and slowly ascended to the top. I do not know how long it took me to reach the halfway mark at the first landing, but I maneuvered my body and my walker gradually up each step, conscious of the added burden I carried. When I got to the top, I entered the prayer room and laid prone, motionless, face down on the carpet, and sobbed while calling on my heavenly Father.

> The Spirit of God has made me, and the breath of
> the Almighty gives me life.
>
> *Job 33:4, (NKJV)*

I needed His breath, His life to revive and encourage me again! Amidst weeping, tears and much grief, all of which I hauled up the stairs, I begged the Lord to answer this question: "Why couldn't I stay with you, Daddy? Why did I have to leave heaven? I want to be with you. I don't want to let go. Show me how to release heaven's grip!" The problem of letting go was tearing me apart. Even as I tried to write my story a month after the hospital release, I grappled, burdened by what it meant, straining to process my loss and feeling out of sorts with the world around me.

Rûach (חוּר) (pronounced ***roo-ahk***) is the Hebrew word meaning "Spirit, wind, breath of the mouth; to breathe out." Some scholars agree *rûach* can also mean "wind of heaven." Whatever the specific meaning in scripture, the word represents the creative breath of God. It was God who hovered over creation at the dawn of time *(Genesis 1:2),* and breathed life into the dust of the ground (*Genesis 2:7*), and formed Adam; just like it was God who breathed life into me and said I would live in spite of medical experts' opinions.

> The earth was without form, and void; and darkness was on the face of the deep. And the Spirit of God was hovering over the face of the waters.
> *(Genesis 1:2, NKJV)*

The "Spirit of God" hovering over the waters can be expressed in the phrase *Rûach Elohim*, (pronounced ***roo-ahk el-o-heem),*** meaning "Spirit of God." Although some deny the Word's identification with the Holy Spirit noted in Christian theology, I do not doubt God can move in this way as I have experienced this phenomenon first hand. As I lay on the floor, I felt His Spirit hovering over me, like a cloud, gently swaying before a burst of rain. His Spirit lingered, shielding me like a blanket suspended above, as if joining in my grief. We rested in this place for a while, and then I heard the Father speak to me. "You have not left heaven, my child. I AM right here! I AM heaven! Heaven is right here with You, Adina. I AM always right here."

Heaven is the various characteristics of God colored in every shade of love that one could possibly imagine, experience or enjoy; and the breath of the Almighty, speaking to me, gave me new life!

God is love *(1 John 4:8).*

Wow! I was undone. I tried to wrap my brain around this new idea. Heaven is not a place built for God, or merely a place we go. Heaven is God and He is heaven. Heaven encompasses wherever He abides. I now know the word heaven means "God" himself. I am at peace knowing no matter where my God abides, heaven's physical location and purpose are found in Him. He is all that - because He is. Heaven is not a place where God lives, but a manifestation of who God is. Heaven is a place where this amazing form of love is expressed, completeness only possible because God is there. Jesus said, "For indeed, the Kingdom of God is within you!" *(Luke 17:21, NKJV).*

The most debilitating melee of all was dealing with the landmine left in my brain, the memories of heaven. I meditated on them constantly, as I pondered the meaning of an experience which stained my mind with indelible ink. I felt so much indescribable grief at the apparent absence of what was formerly the most joyous life episode. Knowing heaven could be as near as my knees brought me comfort and rest. I was able to stop grieving the loss of heaven and began anticipating the joy of what lay ahead.

Personal Perspective

Trying to make sense of all I went through resulted in summarizing many truths. I am not trying to present new doctrine or imply scriptural insights better left to qualified theologians. It is not the desire of anyone connected with the book to be controversial or propose alternative doctrine. As well, we want to be respectful of revelations without adding or taking away from accepted biblical truths. Sharing what I saw and what it meant to me is the purpose of the book. Hopefully you will be inspired by what is shared or the information will lead you to greater insights. May the Lord teach and reveal only HIS truth! My message is mainly that *prayer* did all for me! Francis Frangipane said it beautifully in a collection of his most memorable quotes. Below as taken from his book *Like a Watered Garden:*

Bringing Heaven

The faith Christ inspires
not only brings us
to heaven when we die,
but it is capable of
bringing Heaven
to where we live.
In Christ's Image Training

Prayer helped me find heaven in this existence and the peace I craved. Prayer assisted in coping with my departure from a place so unearthly and remarkable I can hardly wait to return. I want to learn more about the place God has prepared for me and the only way to appease my desire for more is prayer. So I pray! When I feel sad, lost, fearful or lonely, I seek my God, while looking for my part of heaven in the here and now. Knowing He is with me always *(Matthew 28:20)*, He is there in every calamity! He is my peace, my joy and my prayer song.

CHAPTER NINE

The Director's Cut

Because I was not cut off before the darkness,
neither has he covered the deep
darkness from my face.
Job 23:17 (NKJV)

Emergency Room Tragedy

Operating room *mishap* is what made my hospital visit *"outstanding,"* said one doctor. If you have not figured it out yet, my medical crisis was more than a severe case of anaphylaxis or a pierced endotracheal tube. Upon reflection, unraveled events in the ER which have not been fully disclosed yet, seem bizarre at the very least, unbelievable by normal standards and in the extreme, horrifying. If what happened had ended with a mere drive to the hospital and rendered emergency care, this unexceptional story would not likely be repeated. But the theater for the miraculous had been set. All players were in place, including the villain, the background staged, and the props in position. As already noted, I was completely unconscious, my heart stopped, my lungs shut down, and my airway was one-hundred percent restricted. What happened to me in the spirit, only God can say, but my body underwent an outrageous assault! Knowing my poor husband went through this alone breaks my heart. Although we spent quiet times discussing what to do if either of us were ever in a coma (or some similar crisis), I never thought I would encounter life threatening trauma first hand. I am amazed how protectively Trevor stood by. Now I look at him differently with absolute confidence he is the man God chose for me, the one who will carry both me and my daughter through any desert, tragedy or challenge.

Unbelievable

Trevor, in his own words, explains the unfolding scene:

> We arrived at the emergency room trailing behind the ambulance. Medical technicians strapped Adina to a portable gurney and were lowering her unconscious body out the back end of the vehicle. Everything was kind of crazy and I didn't know what I was supposed to be doing. "Hey, that's my wife!" so I followed the EMTs as they ushered her into a reception bay. A nurse led me to a chair with a computer nearby to gather Adina's information. Part of me was trying to focus on remembering our street address, while I kept looking over my right shoulder. Although I really didn't know what was expected, I sensed I needed to keep an eye on Adina. I noticed a sea of colorful nursing gowns, and white coats, roughly a dozen medical personnel. In spite of the urgent atmosphere, staff seemed to work in keenly choreographed and simultaneously organized chaos.
>
> Several times the curtain opened, then closed, then opened again, so I could watch. For obvious privacy reasons a nurse kept pulling the curtain closed,

but I appreciated it left open. Another technician, realizing I was her husband, kept it open. Only slightly ajar, the gap left just enough space for me to see into the hospital bay. I had full view of the room and the people behind me. Hospital records indicated *no* Adina Kring on file, but when they checked for her maiden name, the clerk seemed satisfied. This all happened in the span of about fifteen seconds. After providing basic information, I stepped back and positioned myself at an opportune vantage point. Indistinguishable, the two EMTs grew increasingly anxious.

One standing at the head of her bed said, "We need to get her airway open."

Directing his question to the nurse he asked, "Where's the doctor?"

The nurse replied, "I don't know. He's not here yet."

The same panicked EMT said, "He's got fifteen seconds. If he's not here, I'm going to have to trach her. Is he in the hallway?"

The attending nurse stepped into the hallway for a quick look. Returning rather somberly he spoke. "He's not there. I don't see him."

The other EMT said, "We're losing her. I need to cut her right now."

Fireworks

In the excitement, I learned Adina's heart and lungs had stopped and that she lost consciousness while in the ambulance. It had been roughly ten minutes without oxygen, so I felt every fiber of my being on fire and frozen at the same time. Watching a man with a knife to her throat, no matter how beneficial, was traumatic. As for actual ER events, they seemed like a matrix moment...time kind of halted. I can only describe the emotion, the degree of trauma and the associated agony. Every nerve ending in my body fires when I think about how intense the situation was. I knew what was at stake (everything that mattered in my life) and the decision would be made during the next few seconds. My nervous system was overloaded. It's like experiencing a surge of electricity, painful, disruptive, but endurable... still wholly unpleasant.

Called "direction of care" emergency personnel are required to transfer patient to the doctor upon arrival, but there was no doctor present. The first EMT, who seemed to be in control, recognized Adina's precarious situation. He took matters into his own hands and made a drastic decision.

I saw him open a scalpel and remove the sterile packaging.

As the blade made contact, flashbacks to memories of new prep cooks I trained in the past darted across my mind. EMT 1 took a deep breath and began to make an incision. His face looked committed as if to say, "We're doing this." Then I saw the scalpel connect with her neck and watched in disbelief. Clearly, he made a mistake; it was not a clean cut. I saw what I would describe as *hesitation* while the blade sank into her flesh, leaving a jagged non-fluid cut across the throat. As an experienced cook in the culinary industry for over ten years, I trained many new prep-cooks in meat fabrication. As unfeeling as it may sound, portioning meat is not unlike what was happening right before my eyes. To do it well is a skill one learns. For instance, in order to cut a ribeye to the appropriate size, one would use a long curved, extremely sharp blade called the *scimitar*. To slice a cut of meat, the stroke is one fluid cut, an even movement from top to bottom and the result is a perfect, evenly cut steak. But a common mistake newbies often make in learning how to master this skill is *to saw the meat*, as if cutting a piece of wood, by moving the blade back and forth. To do so leaves marks and messes up the presentation. You want the cut to be flat and even. Often while learning how to mimic this slice in one pass, they make mistakes which result in the same hesitation. So when I saw the EMT's hand jerk as he was cutting Adina's trachea, I knew his reaction was a sign something had gone wrong.

My attention was immediately drawn to EMT 2 who obviously saw the same disturbing thing. His eyes became as wide as dinner plates as he hurried over to ground zero. "Move!" was all he said as he opened a new scalpel and made a second incision. From where I could see, there was not a lot of blood at this point, but in less than three seconds, we were on a crazy anti-gravity rollercoaster. "What…did this guy just do to my wife?" is a question I asked myself, coupled with internal questions as to why he was cutting perpendicularly across her neck rather than vertically? Isn't a tracheotomy performed cutting an incision down the middle of the neck near the clavicle?

Regardless, her airway was open! The cost was great, but her life had been spared, for now! In a group effort, staff lifted her so a compression board could be placed beneath her body. They needed to restart her heart and begin pumping air into the lungs.

Movies and television give a misleading portrayal of CPR. We get the idea resuscitative compressions are nice soft, short bursts of energy. This was the hardest part to watch. To restart her lungs they tried to violently force air into the body. EMT 1 put his hands in the familiar compression position, palm over palm, and began pumping with his full body weight hard and fast in the center of her chest. It looked like he was going to push the sternum back to the spine. Repeatedly, the EMT hammered her chest with his doubled fists. With every forceful downward push her comatose body concaved as her extremities flew upward bouncing like basketballs on the table as she exsanguinated[62] through the slit in her neck. Air moving in and out of the incision caused her to aspirate blood into her lungs, which

---

[62] A medical term used by emergency personnel meaning "to drain of blood." The term is often used to describe the process of bleeding to death.

ultimately caused pneumonia...but that was much later.

Experts say the throat is one of the most prolific bleeding sources. Compressions continued. Each attempt to pump air into the lungs resulted in a terrifying scarlet deluge.[63] Flowing out several lacerations, attending staff became physical targets of the flood. I stood horrified as one of the nurses walked to a small sink, removed his gloves and washed his hands. Water and blood filled the sink basin, swirling down the drain in a spiral descent that washed away any optimism. I wondered is she going to make it. A sudden gasp!

"Is she breathing?"

Beep...beep...beep...beep...beep...beep....

Gasp...exhale... Sigh.

Her heart started!

Soon Dr. Fredy arrived. Immediately recognizing the severity of the situation, he made a medical decision for life-saving surgery. At this point I was removed from the emergency bay. They set me at a nearby desk about five feet outside the room where Adina lay, possibly dying, and closed the curtain again so I could no longer see what was happening. They asked me to wait there. Shortly, someone began asking questions about Adina's medical

---

[63] Meaning red flood.

history and wanted a detailed description clarifying what happened prior to hospital arrival. Someone came to me and said, "We will be with you in a minute." I waited until a female physician came to speak with me (not sure of her role), but she said Adina was being rushed to surgery. She escorted me to a private conference room near the lobby of the ER. When I arrived, Pastor Rae joined me and I shared what transpired. Hours later, I learned EMT 1 had cut her left external jugular vein almost all the way through. The external jugular is smaller than the internal jugular and runs closer to the surface of the skin, which was the cause of all the plasma coming from her nose and mouth.

Depending on which artery is cut a patient can bleed to death in as little as two minutes.

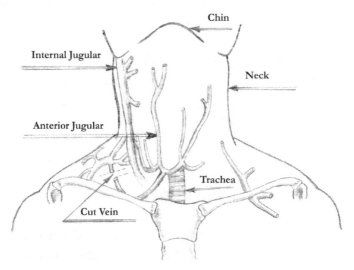

FIG. 9-1: A drawing showing the location of the vein cut during emergency room rescue efforts. (Artist Antonio M. Delgado. Used with permission).

This image demonstrates where the incision was made at the base of the neck just above the clavicle bone left of center. Trevor continues:

> Our friends and Christian family (Pastor Rae, Jacque R, Johnnie F, Edwin A, and his mother Isabel) joined me in the conference room where we all took turns alternating between prayers and tears. Admitted to the surgical ICU, Rae and I were also moved to another conference room where we remained for a couple hours until surgery ended. We sat hopeful for any further word from the attending physician.

There were so many intricate pieces and many witnesses. Looking back I see his perspective and how Trevor stood on patrol watching over the orchestration of every detail. Dr. Fredy, the physician who pinched and held my jugular vein closed as they wheeled me into surgery spoke with Trevor who recalled their conversation.

> "How did she get here?" Dr. Fredy asked, and then paused he added, "Trying to save her life they slit her jugular."

> Trevor looked pasty. As the blood drained from his face, leaving only traces of confusion amidst pandemonium, he swallowed hard. "I don't know what…happened. They almost killed her!"

Pastor Rae, also in shock, could not believe only hours before we were ministering together and now I was in the fight of my life. Boldly, the doctor just laid out the details.

The Grim Report

"Listen, here's what happening," said Dr. Fredy, "It is very grim. I don't know if she'll make it through the night. So, I'm not going to give you a lot of hope."

A tearful Trevor overwhelmed with grief cried so much that day, and needed to have the Lord's bravest, strongest and mightiest warriors to counteract the doctor's report. Here he shares more:

> While we waited, I made a call to LaNora Morin, the person we call our spiritual mother, a minister of the faith and someone whom we embrace as more than family, a mentor, a trainer, an equipper, and someone who has loved us. As a mighty woman of God and effective intercessor, she is the warrior we knew would be able to put a hedge of prayer around Adina. LaNora came down from Phoenix the next day. But for those first important moments on the phone, she promised to make some calls and get more intercessors praying. So Pastor Rae and I continued to pray and talk. Hours later, LaNora called back and said she contacted the *K Family*, a couple I have known since I was young. At the time, they headed up the prayer portion of a group called *Transform Tucson*. Through prayer, outreach and acts of mercy throughout town, this family ministered to many in the community. It was primarily a prayer group, but they were known for performing acts of service where support and help were desperately needed. As friends and partners with LaNora, they joined the prayer effort. Shortly afterwards, Rich and Maryanne K, were on their way to the hospital. Rich is a retired pulmonologist. As a physician who specialized in the proper

function and complications associated with the lungs, I asked if he could explain what the doctors were not making clear. He said asthma can slowly and unnoticeably restrict the airway, while allergic reactions can affect the lungs. Putting these two conditions together with the commotion in the ER, the situation created a *perfect storm* of anarchy.

Because of the wretched particulars corrective medical surgery was inevitable and involved correcting two incisions. Dr. Robert D had to seal both the trach and the gash on my neck, remove three damaged trachea rings, and repair a severed artery and vocal chord. He also removed cartilage supposedly no longer needed. He noted there was a profuse amount of bleeding from my neck, as my jugular vein had been severed. He needed to tie off the vessel, including my thyroid gland and enteral tracheal which were also bleeding. Dr. Robert explains what tasks he performed and why:

What the medical team was really trying to do was make an incision between the thyroid cartilage and cricoid-cartilage, a procedure known as *cricothyrotomy*. This is an incision through the skin and the cricothyroid[64] membrane used for emergency relief of upper respiratory obstructions. But they cut below the cricoid-cartilage, actually performing a tracheostomy, which is to create an artificial opening through the neck into the trachea. [Due to critical condition at time of presenting in ER this was a fateful situation].

---

[64] Known in laymen's terms as the "windpipe."

Basically, Dr. Robert performed a revision of the tracheostomy caused by a slashed tracheotomy, and also put an endotracheal tube into my neck. Due to swelling, he said, he was not able to intubate me and go through the mouth, as would be normal procedure. I was intubated in the operating room, while my stats continued to drop. It became necessary to secure my airway as it had been "compromised" (as they say in the medical field).

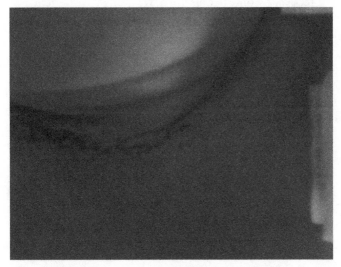

PHOTO 9-2: Aerial view of the corrective incision
on Adina's neck made by Dr. Robert D.

"Adina's blood welled out her mouth and nose," said Dr. Robert. "The only thing she had going for her was her age." Realizing I was younger than most patients presenting with such a severe a case of anaphylaxis, he felt I could probably tolerate more than an older person in the same situation. Dr. Robert continues his explanation:

> Her oxygen levels became very low. If she was able
> to survive, my long term assessment was very poor.
> Even in the operating room, we were able to get
> her stats [oxygen levels] into the high eighties. We

decreased her ability to saturate, got the tube out, and controlled the bleeding, but we were looking at forty-five minutes with airway issues. At the very least we expected significant neurological damage (what doctors call *sequela*, a secondary consequence of the lack of oxygen). The younger and healthier you are, the better chance you have of complete recovery. Some people are never going to experience full recovery. She has neurological issues dealing with weakness and strength in her arms and legs. As for the long term affects from initial trauma, only time will tell. But I have always been impressed with her recovery. She has a great soul and good fighting spirit.

Dr. Robert, who believes in miracles, said he considered my recovery an absolute wonder. "Adina is a person of faith and me being a person of faith, certainly on that day, all things worked out the way they should," he said.

No Protocol

From that nearly deadly day, it would be two weeks before I was released, cut loose from hospital mayhem. On Thursday night, February 16th, I was asked to go for a walk around the ICU. Stunned, I sat seriously contemplating the idea. Reluctantly, I said "yes." I took a cool couple of laps with the aid of a walker. "I'm not gonna' lie." It was hard, painful and meticulous. I had been bedridden since arriving and muscles had atrophied. Friday morning the medical team said I was well enough to move to a patient room. Arriving at my *new crib* around 9 a.m., what to do next was not clear. Once the doctors decided to remove the trach tube, I became an anomaly. They did not have protocols in place to care for someone in my condition, mainly because no one had ever been in a similar situation or presented the same set of unusual circumstances. Later the same day, one of the doctors in my treatment team asked if I wanted to go home. I said, "YES!" Once out of the drug induced paralysis, I was only in the hospital for another week. Shortly before being released, Dr. Hannah came by to see how I was doing:

> A few days following [the second] surgery,[65] I went to her room to check on her. She was actually getting ready to leave the hospital and that was quiet remarkable. Thinking she would still be sick in the ICU, I certainly was not expecting to find her up and preparing for discharge.

Releasing me seemed like a better choice than guessing at a care plan. Once hospital staff began debating discharge particulars, I did not know what to expect. But without hesitation, I consented. I wanted to quit hospital life, clearly an answer to prayer. I was not concerned with the reasons, just happy to be leaving, still with lots of questions. Doctors requested a few tests, explained a few things, had me fill-out some paperwork, and at 2:42 p.m., discharged me. The trauma was behind and I wanted, no I needed, to quickly get back to normal life. What I did not realize was although my healing was pretty miraculous and amazingly fast, I was still not fully recuperated and wholeness was not instantaneous. Going home proved that point. I was not able to walk and went outside the house only in a wheelchair. Although this is likely a TMI[66] moment, normal body functions had not fully returned. Equilibrium was gone, as was my depth perception and ability to do even the simplest tasks. Future prognoses included some disturbing negative possible

---

[65] Dr. Hannah D was the ER anesthesiologist, and again for the second surgery when Dr. Robert D removed the tracheal tube.

[66] TMI is an abbreviation for the phrase meaning: "too much information."

outcomes: kidney failure, tremors, falling down, loss of hand and eye coordination, imbalance, memory loss, and vocal chord alternation affecting my ability to sing.

Dr. David T noted, I am lucky, but would have to stay healthy and fit. I continue to have periodic appointments with Dr. Robert D to revisit the neck wound, and to ensure scar tissue does not form (a condition called subglottic stenosis[67]), which could further restrict my airway. I accept something extraordinary took place. But most amazing of all was when we realized *The Director's Cut* came twice: once when He used *trachea tragedy* to guide my restoration and again when I was **cut** from the hospital roster and sent home because only God could heal me from what was to come!

> "[God] reached down from heaven and rescued me"
> *(Psalms 18:16, NLT).*

My first real taste of freedom came when my husband and two body guards, [dear brothers who wanted to ensure my comfort and safety], wheeled me into the Sunday service; and for a few short, but oh so glorious minutes, I shared with my Christian family the love of God, whose touch was still more than mere memory.

The perception has always been that this spectacle was a demonic attack. Due to the previous explanation, I understand everyone's confusion, but I never felt the near death experience was demonic like so many others trying to cope with the meaning of this whole fiasco. I always believed that it was God giving the people an opportunity to understand how prayer is a vehicle that can change any circumstance from trouble to triumph!

---

[67] Although rare, acquired **subglottic stenosis** is generally the result of a problematic airway intubation or a result of a life-threatening airway emergency.

CHAPTER TEN

The Machine

Look, I tell you, lift up your eyes, and see that the
fields are white for harvest.
John 4:35 (ESV)

From the moment Dr. Cynthia told me I could not stay in heaven, the dreaded process of letting go began. Goodbye to the beauty, the love, peace, joy, the powerful presence and newly discovered keener awareness of the *Spirit of Glory*. I began initiating a painful journey which involved **letting go of heaven**! I knew I was not dead, still releasing how I felt and what it all looked like was a difficult task; one I did not understand and only cooperated with reluctantly. Before departing, the Lord gave me a personal message and another, which I believe is my commission to share with all believers, the details of which I have done my best to delineate in the following narrative. Please note while trying to communicate the imagery, I do not want to interpret or misinterpret God's message. Although likely impossible, I will do my best to convey the details without prejudice while trying to give the best possible portrayal so you may interpret it for yourself. I pray the Lord guides you.

Cliffhanger

Safe and surrounded by the protection of the Lord, I experienced what can only be depicted as the *Holy Spirit* supporting from behind. The Lord took us to where I stood on a cliff overlooking land as far as the eye could see. Without any effort, I was instantly transported to a higher place looking out at another unknown wonder. Off in the distance, I observed a most peculiar sight. The dictionary describes a machine as "an apparatus consisting of interrelated parts with separate functions, used in the performance of some kind of work." What a perfect explanation of what I saw. I witnessed some sort of mechanical contraption and beneath the equipment what looked like a meadow, a field *white for harvest*,[68] being sheared by a *combine harvester*, a huge modern day machine used to gather crops.

Contemplating, I realized my *combine* was an optical illusion, a double image that tricked the eye. The machine appeared to be moving like a locomotive with the wheels of a train, driven by a sort of piston motion, but the base was wider than a train, almost triple in size. This up and down piston action was a type of motor propelling the machine onward. It moved like a wheat thresher pulling in an entire field in a single rotation, cutting, threshing, and cleaning the crops in one smooth maneuver. The Lord spoke indicating this **thing** is "*The People*" functioning like a machine, but not like a metal structure (even though that is how it appeared). I saw slow gears gradually grinding as if farming the land. I later felt the Lord gave me a message for YOU. This symbolic imagery was intended to convey His greater meaning and higher intention for all we are to do here on earth.

Closer examination revealed to my amazement the machine was made up of people, not a machine at all. They were like circus acrobats entwined and tumbling in unison as they appeared to be taking plots of land, symbolically taking territory absorbing what

---

[68] John 4:35

was beneath the wheels of the train and making what once appeared to be fields of wheat blowing in the wind, a functioning part of the greater machine. Metaphorically, the fields were being harvested for people—not grains of wheat—to add to God's beautiful kingdom of purpose and love. Becoming a believer is how you become part of the machine, God's instrument made of people, moving forward for His intent and purpose. The unity never ignored the importance, the individuality or the function of each person. It was a machine built on love, trust and relationship. The unified goal was to take more territory for the kingdom of God. This mechanism moved sluggishly, and kept stopping. I remember being irritated by the constant interruptions. Each stop, every step, exemplified God's love. "His grace **is** sufficient and his power made perfect in weakness" *(2 Corinthians 12:9)*. In other words, His power is flawless in spite of our frailty because it requires us to rely on God; not the strength of our flesh. God is exulted as we rise above our weaknesses through His greatness and mercy.

Each Man's Role

My reputation has been one of a harvester, a servant committed to seeing the lost won for Jesus. Many Christians take the position "I don't need to witness today; after all, Adina is the one with the evangelistic call." I think the Lord was trying to show me we all need to commit to bringing people into the body of believers. People are added to the body so they can be made well. Once they are well again they become part of *The Machine* and begin to win souls for the kingdom. He also began to show me the roles of each man. Every person has a part to play and their job helps to advance the kingdom. No matter what your role, no matter how small or insignificant you think your assignment, all duties are equal and on level playing ground. Everyone is responsible for their part in making the machine function. Just like the definition of *"machine,"* **_the people_** are like an apparatus consisting of interrelated parts with separate functions, used in performing God's work. Advancing the kingdom is paramount to the Lord because He wants all to come to Him, and none to be lost *(2 Peter 3:9)*. We should ask ourselves, "Am I the one interrupting the flow of God's Kingdom, goal and purpose?"

Prior to the incident, the Lord revealed a comparison between the church and a hospital. Everyone needs some level of healing. Some are in a hospital bed receiving ministry for wounds inflicted by participation in the world's disorder. Some are in surgery because their wounds are life threatening, intensive care for those who need constant and direct treatment, or maybe they are merely in urgent care, getting a quick fix, a new in-filling of the Spirit and back to work. But we are all being healed at different times and for different reasons. God's work in our lives here on earth involves individualized therapy. He wants to heal us so we can be integrated into His Machine in order to build His Kingdom.

If your role is to change diapers or you are the one who speaks from the platform, each person's job is equal in the sight of God. Nothing and no one is more important than any other! There is much work to do. But road blocks will stop progress, so God must intervene. By road blocks, I mean human behaviors like bitterness, disobedience, deceit, backbiting, offenses, coveting others' positions: basic issues of the heart. More simply, the ruined or ungodly condition of the heart will stop the advancement of God's kingdom. If someone is not doing their job, the Lord will fix the problem by eventually removing them from the machine's purpose because that person disconnected from the two greatest commandments: "to love the Lord your God with all your heart, soul, mind and strength and to love your neighbor as yourself."[xxv]

Indifference also causes the *machine's* interruptions and affects kingdom expansion. But the work continues and the machine must resume its course. The Lord's efforts are always aiding the movement of the machine, but He never loses sight of the individual's need for greater healing. We should not keep our Christian status secret when in the marketplace; same for the classroom, the stay-at-home mom doing the laundry, or for someone just buying groceries. Even the CEO must go to the four corners of their world (their own mission field) and preach the gospel. If you think your job is minuscule, you are wrong! Each person and what we do, where we serve is important. Only you can do what God has purposed for you and there is no do-over; that moment is gone! You will need to be removed from the machine, healed by the Potter's hand and then returned to minister at a later date. Can you see the compassion of our God who sees all? Generally, people do not understand how important their role is. Everybody has a call on their life. Each person is so central to the advancement of the kingdom, but we need to know striving and murmuring stops the machine from going forward. Everyone has been strategically placed to connect with someone, but the enemy wants to disrupt your progress; to stop your role being played out to the fullest.

Cogs in the Machine

In practical terms, here's an application of this vision. I was introduced to a fresh new face, Nerissa R, a returning convert who had just begun coming to GTTN. So often I am introduced to people who are considering a Christian lifestyle. They are not fully in the kingdom, nor are they back in the world. I love these kinds of mission opportunities. It is awesome to witness the Lord's healing power and changing grace in the lives of the newly converted believer. But if the Lord does not specifically inspire me, I refuse to move ahead. I do not want to waste my time working with people the Lord has not prepared for me, so I asked the Lord, "What do you want me to do with her?" I know this sounds cold, but I always have to be about my Father's business *(Luke 2:49)*. There are so many distractions when you serve the Lord, and I have to be careful to only do those things that will keep the machine (God's purposes) moving forward. When I inquired about her, the Lord said, "Draw her near. Bring her close." As she and I became friends, I wanted to be sure she was comfortable at Grace. At the time, we had a church with about twelve-hundred attenders and large church membership can be intimidating. It is easy to get lost, fail to connect or find your niche, or worse, never unite with the family. I wanted to make sure she was plugged-in.

"When Adina scooped me up and nurtured me like a mom, our friendship felt like home," said Nerissa. "The flame was in me, but meeting Adina sparked the passion of my love for Jesus and ignited my return from the world to heavenly devotion planted within me at an early age."

Nerissa's introduction to the machine was seamless and without conflict. She is now a part of something bigger, better, and more meaningful. My job was to make sure she found her place in the cogs which drive the mechanisms of the heavenly work God sets us to do. When God has to step in to fix things, it means you are side-lined and He has to replace a section of the machine with a willing soul. I have heard it said, "God is not tolerant;" after all, He allowed evil men to crucify His only son *(John 3:16)*. No, "God is not tolerant; He is merciful and ***longsuffering!***"[69] The machine keeps working, slowly grinding as it moves forward. Because Nerissa was willing and open to becoming part of a harvesting church, she quickly found her place in the machine's inner structure and began to go to work.

Another practical application of serving God and the machine looks like my interaction with the woman I met in the mall. Three months after the incident, I was trying to buy an Easter dress for my daughter. I saw a woman across the store and felt an *impression* from the Lord to speak to her. I hesitated because, "Well, you know…was

---

[69] **Longsuffering:** Meaning "enduring injury, trouble, or provocation long and patiently." Only a loving Father would do so in light of evil works and acts of hatred. He gives us every opportunity to repent and return to Him. (Definition derived from online dictionary.com).

that just me? Is that you Lord? Am I going to trust Him? We get caught up in our own thinking: 'will I look foolish?'" This woman and I made very real eye contact. For just a moment, I returned to the clothes I had been shuffling through on the rack in front of me. When I looked up again, it was awkward. You know how you are talking to someone with your eyes. I said "Hi" and she walked away.

I thought, "Oh God, I can't let this woman walk away." I chased her into the mall court.

"Hey, excuse me." She turned around.

"I'm sorry, but I noticed you were looking at me."

"Yah," she continued, "No, I thought you were going to say something."

Then I said, "Yeah, I was. I was going to say something, but I'm sorry I didn't. I just wanted to tell you Jesus loves you and cares about your situation and what you're going through." Then I asked, "Can I pray for you?"

She erupted into tears and said, "Yes!"

I do this kind of thing all the time. Actually, these eternal opportunities happen to us all, but often these incredible moments are not recognized. We must listen and learn to react according to His wishes. Doing this type of "stop, drop and roll" ministry (you know, working to put the fire out) is something I am known for and often did before the incident, although only when I felt like it. Sometimes I would feel the Lord pressing me and I would be obedient, but now I jump at the opportunity because I carry this constant feeling of urgency. I gave her a card and invited her to church, encouraging her to call anytime.

Blind Man's Bluff

Last observation of *The Machine,* I was looking down at an oddly prophetic image watching it move towards the horizon where it eventually disappeared. Instantly I moved from the bluff, floating from this high place, a perfect vantage point, to a lower level with a totally different view. I was back where I first opened my eyes and encountered Cynthia. Throughout what I can only call a forewarning vision, Cynthia never left me. She guided me during the entire heavenly visit. When the Lord spoke, she would pull back. When I was on the bluff, she was waiting behind, always smiling and always *knowing.* I did not see her, but knew she was there. This revelation is something I still deal with today. As with my heavenly guide, I am always trying to share what I learned from Cynthia's example. We must remember the Lord and honor Him, glorify Him in all we do. Cynthia recognized the sovereignty of God: supreme, powerful, all knowing; lofty with imposing authority. Majestic! When encountering ministry moments, I try to bring my newest progeny to the same realization about who God truly is. I want to say to them, "I've brought you to the bluff, look out and tell me what you see? Where is Jesus?" Do they see what God is doing?

Perplexing Purpose

The knowledge of God's intervention in our world brings peace, but I wrestle with the purpose of my horrific ordeal. I know God does nothing (or rather allows nothing to happen) without purpose. Scripture tells us, "He uses all things…for good" *(Romans 8:28).* But unlike many who believe God will *do* bad things to them for some greater purpose, I do not believe that is how God's economy works. He is perfect, He is love, He is great and virtuous! My prayer is:

Show me Lord what you want me to say or do with what I witnessed. What is your heart? And what do you say about the matter?

Heavenly Separation

The heaviness of leaving heaven began to press on my heart like an immoveable weight. The pain, a dull but severe heartache--like the loss of love, devastating and unrelenting--hung over my soul like a storm cloud of inevitable despair. Yet, I knew I was exiting heaven when the Power of the Highest[70] who had been overshadowing me stepped back and instantly I was down among the people who began to crowd around me. I never got a chance to thank Cynthia or say goodbye. Our eyes never shared a farewell. I wish I had more time. Maybe saying goodbye was not important because she knows she will see me again.

At the moment of separation, thousands upon thousands of people urgently shuffled towards me, each with a message. It was a crowd, but no crowding. No one was a male or female, no color, like black, white, or brown, no Baptist, no Catholic, no Hebrew or any other delineation that would segregate them. The different tribes and tongues were not the focus of this throng. It was their spirits relating and speaking to me, although speech was not necessary. We were all in one accord.[xxvi] I felt unified, connected with their spirits. All the physical stuff seemingly fell off their bodies. Still, with hands they pressed their thoughts towards me, on to me and into me. I felt them saying things like: "Remember this" and "Don't forget what's truly important." The people were not exactly expressing doubts, but rather examples of "I shoulda', woulda', coulda'." This knowledge is a constant reminder of what they wanted me to understand and to share with others. Even now when in prayer, the memory of one of the hands will come again (not unlike a gentle tapping on the

---

[70] The Holy Ghost is another name for The Holy Spirit. See *Luke 1:35, (KJV)*.

shoulder) to touch my spirit, reminding and warning. I feel their sorrow, dare I say regret?

> "Adina don't forget." The words haunt me and echo into space like a soft reverberation emanating from my mind, very eerie and ethereal at the same time.

> "I wish I had spoken to my brother about the Lord."

> "Like David, I wish I had danced more before God."

> "If only I'd made more time to pray with others."

> "Why didn't I tell my friend about Jesus and His plan for salvation?"

Messages of remorse, for lack of a better term, warned me not to be consumed by *stuff*. Do not let your stuff take the place of God in your heart. Where are you with your stuff? If it displaces the Lord's throne in your life, then stuff becomes a problem and your life feels troubled. When in heaven, nothing else really matters. We get wrapped up with our clothes, shoes, even our bodies. At the end of the day what kind of car you drive is not important to the Lord. Remember what is! Expressed feelings of grief were caused by regrets for the lost—the people—the unsaved, those in their sphere of influence, not about their stuff. These people were seemingly brokenhearted over what they did not do [thus *The Machine*]. In heaven there is a fullness of joy, a profound peace, but as I was leaving everyone tried to remind me to be in the world, not of the world. "Do not love the world or the things of the world," *(1 John 2:15, ESV)*. They warned me to take this posture and to be impassioned, committed to arriving in heaven having completed the tasks set before me by the Lord. "I don't want to be the one who says, "woulda', shoulda', coulda'." I want to fulfill the purpose the Lord has for me here on earth. It is not about building my own kingdom. We are called to build His. Later after I was resuscitated, I asked the Lord during prayer, "Why did you show this to me? What am I supposed to do with this information?"

> Therefore, since we are surrounded by so great a cloud of witnesses, let us also lay aside every weight, and sin which clings so closely, and let us run with endurance the race that is set before us, looking to Jesus, the founder and perfecter of our faith, who for the joy that was set before him endured the cross, despising the shame, and is seated at the right hand of the throne of God.
>
> *Hebrews 12:1-2 (ESV)*

God does nothing without purpose. He is always speaking, saying something, and trying to communicate with His people. There is such seriousness about the call and work of God. I am compelled to keep my eyes on the kingdom and His will. I plan to do so for my entire life:

> Do not love the world or the things in the world. If anyone loves the world, the love of the Father is not in him. For all that is in the world— the desires of the flesh and the desires of the eyes and pride in possessions—is not from the Father but is from the world. And the world is passing away along with its desires, but whoever does the will of God abides forever.
>
> *1 John 2:15-17, (ESV)*

An Invitation for All

Sometimes when I am in worship, I feel transported into the presence of God, which takes my breath away. Simple things, everyday things (a baby's eyes, your husband's arms, a beautiful day, the Grand Canyon, watching birds soar across the sky, or butterflies hovering over a golden Arizona poppy with its bright orange basal spot) all reminders of being home in heaven. These moments give me a glimpse and then God does not feel so far away.

One day not long after returning home from the hospital, I went to the prayer chapel to speak to the Lord. While there, I once again felt the hands of the crowd, pressing in, "Adina remember. Don't forget." Instantly I was transported to the vision of *The Machine* and the people with their prayer needs. Clearly I was confused. What does it mean Lord? Struggling with letting go and acclimating myself to home life, I prayed I could feel God's presence enter my space and commune with me. I drew near to Him and He drew nearer to me. I felt the same feeling, the heavenly ***knowing*** and suddenly realized ***I was in the presence of God***! My prayers became peaceful and untroubled. When I hear a scripture such as *John 3:27,* "A man can receive nothing except it be given him from heaven" *(KJV),* the meaning of this verse becomes clear. Put simply, nothing comes to us except God gives it. I believe He encouraged and comforted me during some difficult prayer times. Unfortunately, the further away from the incident, the more the spirit of the world tries to rush back into my memories replacing that familiar feeling of ***knowing*** fully and not having to read between the lines. I want to do all in love and ignore the dysfunction of this world. I want to stay close to the Lord, but human nature takes over, and our flesh begins to take control: we fight with our husband, say something catty to someone who cuts us off in traffic, or speak harshly to our children. I do not want the flesh to have dominion over my choices, but still I wear this earth-suit and it affects my walk by weighing down my spirit, and interfering in my time with the Lord. Even simple everyday moments like witnessing to a woman who needs to hear that God loves her can transport me into the *Presence*. At that instant, I am part of *The Machine* doing my portion to introduce the kingdom of God into reality for myself and others. Once again this stellar moment takes my breath away.

During my hospital time I was forced to transition from a heavenly world back into this one. I regrettably put on my earth-suit, one painful sleeve after the other, moving to zip it up; flexing my wrists to pull the hoodie-like flesh over the back of my skull and onto my face while striding toward His Spirit. I know we move from glory to glory.[xxvii] Our efforts should take us away from fallen human nature and lead towards a godlier one. Because I cannot find words to fully describe what I saw or felt, this explanation, which may seem like rambling at times, is the best I can do to convey heaven. I pray the Lord will speak to you through the message. Like an emotional eruption that cannot be contained without another explosion trying to merge into this infinite rush of joyful sensation, these words must suffice. Memories like these are impossible to put into better comprehensible language. Meanwhile, to return to heaven is one of my greatest longings. Next, the greatest desire would be for no one to perish *(2 Peter 3:9)*, but for all to experience *heaven* for themselves. Eternity is a place surrounded by the perfect love of God with unlimited ways to express your love, encircled by those whom you know and love also. Now that would truly be heaven! I hope everyone does all to become part of *The Machine*, so they too will see and experience God and more!

CHAPTER ELEVEN

Miraculous Inspiration

By Laura Steffens

And many of the people believed on him,
and said, "When Christ comes,
Will he do more miracles than these?"
John 7:31 (NKJV)

Adina is favored, but so are any who embrace God's freely offered love. Her story relates to all lives while hopefully directing us towards a closer relationship with the *Miraculous One* who daily demonstrates His power. To this book loaded with mini-stories of friends intersecting Adina's narrative, all relaying particulars of what happened; I add my voice to speak about what she cannot and give testimony of what God has done. Examination of the story and often unbelievable minutiae involves questions. Here we attempt to examine some of these events in lieu of the unexplainable!

Expecting Miracles

To have a chapter implying miracles in a book where every page shares something astonishing seems redundant. But there were so many additional events which had to be told, so this section was created. Miracles are defined as "extraordinary events which surpass all known powers and can only be ascribed to supernatural causes."[71] As believers, Jesus said, "we will do even greater miracles than He has done."[xxviii] Yet we often fail to believe miracles are possible. We should expect God's intervention in His children's lives, He does, after all, exist in the supernatural realm. Prophesy means to declare or predict by divine intervention.[72] When events, visions or words illustrate something supernatural, believers should take notice. Pastor Rae had a vision we feel was rightly deciphered, even though we did not comprehend the full meaning at the time. Here pastor shares what she saw:

> Five days into the ordeal I had a revelation from God. We had been told by hospital staff [as evidenced via medical records, MRIs and CT scans] Adina definitely experienced brain damage and would never be the same if she survived. From the moment it happened, she was surrounded by people needing me to be their shepherd. Adina was also my friend, but I had to be strong for Trevor, her family, and all the babes in the church who feared they were losing this powerful woman in their lives. I spent a day allowing myself to weep. I stayed home from the hospital grieving as I cried out to the Lord. Later I saw a vision of a grand old tree.

---

[71] *From online dictionary.com.*

[72] Ibid.

FIG. 11-1: A drawing of the tree. (Artist Antonio
M. Delgado. Used with permission).

It was as though I looked straight on and could see
trunk and branches simultaneously, the root system
below and the branches above ground, both equal
in size. But the branches and roots were corrupted
and gnarly on the ends, while the central core of
the tree remained healthy. Corrosive elements had
corrupted the tree eating away sections, leaving
no pathway to speak of for transporting life to the

extremities of the sapling. The tree looked limited, heavy and pulled down. I asked the Lord in my spirit, "What is this?" He told me to "speak life into the electrical impulses." It meant nothing to me, nothing at all. But I obeyed. So I said, "I speak life into the electrical impulses in this tree." I saw a light spring through the core moving through the tree branches. These small minute lights were randomly firing. The light went into the trunk and down into the root system flitting about like a butterfly.

I didn't understand this vision, but I knew it was about Adina. God told me to speak life into the branches. Later that night, I met with Trevor. He asked to speak with me alone so we could pray together. Afterwards, Trevor shared he needed someone with whom to process the disastrous events of the emergency room. We declared healing in the name of Jesus. Then he shared the physician's commentary. The neurologist told him Adina experienced global brain damage. He also said, remarkably her interior functions were all there but corroded across the entire surface of the brain. It was as if the nerve endings mimicked the tree where the branches and roots had withdrawn and shriveled. In this damaged condition, neural synapses[73] were unable to connect or grow due to deterioration. As he was speaking, I saw in my mind's eye the image of a tree rotating into horizontal position until it was parallel with the ground. Immediately realizing the tree represented the two lobes of the brain, God told me to speak life into Adina's brain.

---

[73] Loosely meaning: nerve ending connections.

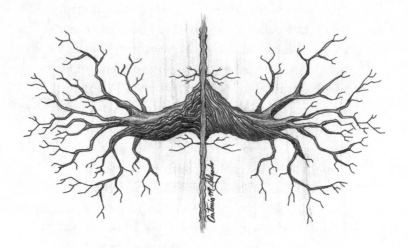

FIG. 11-2: Same drawing, but now as an image of the brain. (Artist Antonio M. Delgado. Used with permission).

"I can't believe you're saying this to me cause the neurologist revealed the neural pathways of the brain were like the branches of a tree" Trevor said. The right and left hemisphere were represented in tree physiology. This visual just made sense. The Lord told us not to accept the doctor's report as final, but to speak life into the neural pathways. The vision looked like a tree with lights firing, flickering and twinkling at the ends of the branches and roots. God was healing Adina's root system by touching her brain. The Lord said, "Speak to the branches and they will live." I proposed, touched by the hand of God, the brain was healed and restored. It started to grow, while nerve endings were reconnected and healed. In my vision, the branches were not blackened, burnt or tarred, [they were withered], making the reward pathways unable to network. But we spoke to the neural connections and told the brain synapses to begin firing. It was so important to do just as the Lord had said.

I began to pray very aggressively. I asked the Lord to heal her, not to keep her alive to be a vegetable or diminished in capacity. I also spoke scriptures declaring she would be like the tree of life: "Blessed is the tree planted by the rivers of water that brings forth fruit in season, whose leaf shall not wither, and whatever she does shall prosper. Even the heat of the sun will not scorch the tree. The righteous shall be like a tree and she shall not wither"[74] We began to speak to the tree of her brain. "The tree of life is the brain," we declared. We had no idea what that meant, but all the same we spoke over her in faith. As I began to pray those words, God showed me Adina's brain, so I would prophesy and pray life to all those neural pathways. There is power in the *Word* of the Lord. Later that night I went to her hospital bed and laid hands on her head. I began to speak to her brain stating it would be fully restored.

In the pastor's example of faith-filled prayer, we see the *Word of God* being played out in reality during a mystifying situation. Simply put, we only need pray, lay hands on the sick, and believe God for a miracle:

> "And these signs will follow those who believe: In [Jesus'] name they will…lay hands on the sick, and they will recover."
>
> *Mark 16:17-18, (NKJV)*

---

[74] Psalms 1:3

As the saying goes, miracles (like people) come in all shapes and sizes. I think there are those miraculous events where God intercedes and mountains are moved, and then there are the daily miracles we witness all the time, exclaiming, *"What a coincidence."* For example, you bump into an old friend you have not seen in years, you find $20 in your pocket, or you get a phone call from someone who accidentally dialed you. Adina always likes to say, "Is it odd or is it God?" God is in those moments as well. We often fail to give credit to the Creator, preferring to find a scientific explanation, or ignore the obvious rather than thanking the Lord for intervening in our lives.

> Adina speaks for herself. "What had I experienced? Did I see heaven? Was it a dream, a nightmare, something my mind created? I do not believe the doctors had any definite or tangible answers, but inquiries were made to find possible explanations outside the obvious that God had performed a miracle!"

Understanding this concept is central to what those most closely involved believe is the final analysis. Dr. Robert D was adamant about the fact it was unlikely Adina heard anything or could have responded to outside stimulus while anesthetized. This truth just makes her visions of heaven even more miraculous. This is what the doctor wrote:

> With the amount of sedation she ultimately had, there is no way she could be hearing things from an outside source or actually recall anything. What she experienced people might argue is just your brain having vivid dreams, but external source of stimulus is not likely. Not one of my patients has been able

to say they were awake in the OR [operating room]. It is impossible to say [medically] what someone's brain is actually doing or whether or not she had a true spiritual or other-worldly experience.

Looking for the Lord in the miraculous should be a daily task for every true believer. Why not? We serve a miracle working God.[xxix] He loves us and every other person on this planet which is a pretty miraculous gift.

A New Name

Another of the most peculiar aspects of Adina's case was the remarkable recovery made in such short time. Dr. Robert D agreed, stating how unusual it is for someone to come back from a prolonged period of low oxygen saturation without experiencing complications. It is unusual because most similar patients have significant problems with recovery, are wheelchair bound, or suffer with stroke-like symptoms, such as paralysis, dizziness, loss of muscle control, seizures, trouble with speech and moody behavior.

Trevor had a thought regarding miracles:

> God is not interested in performing a miracle *for us* so much as He is in teaching us the *process* of miracles, and multiplying them *through us*. Like the old Chinese proverb that says, "Give a man a fish, feed him for a day. Teach a man to fish, feed him for a lifetime." Modified it would sound something like: "Give a miracle and receive momentary gratitude. Teach someone the nature of miracles, and they will learn to miraculously operate through the *person*, *power*, and *presence* of God."

With this understanding, prognosis chatter included statements like: "she might not make it; she'll be a vegetable; she won't be able to walk or speak; she will have to live at a rehabilitation center; she might have trouble walking, talking and remembering things; perhaps her personality will still be there; and finally, her recovery is nothing short of miraculous." Professionals did not say recovery is rare; rather they noted it simply does not happen! Medicine kept her stable, but prayer and the Healer systematically restored her. By the time she was discharged, medical staff referred to her as "the miracle lady."

In response to this nickname, Adina comments, "To be called *'the miracle lady'* is a little humbling, especially since I did nothing to further my own recovery prior to exiting the hospital. I can only recall this chapter of my life with stunned disbelief at how great is our God! The words of a beloved hymn linger in my mind:"

> *How great is our God – sing with me*
> *How great is our God – and all will see*
> *How great, how great is our God*
> > Lyrics by Chris Tomlin, Jesse Reeves,
> > and Ed Cash (2004)

Questionable Circumstances

God wants to intervene in our lives, but not ALL people are healed. So why heal Adina and not others? Many people speculate about God's reasons for allowing strange things to happen, but the results are often flawed. Some of the "why" queries in life will never be answered this side of heaven. Questioning aspects of this nightmare would become on ongoing dialogue in Adina's recovery. But one reality holds true and that is we cannot judge God's love based on our circumstances. The Word says His thoughts and ways are higher than ours (*Romans 11:34*, NLT).

Shortly after Adina's return to church, a woman who sadly just lost her own daughter in a tragic death only months before, came to her asking *why*. "Why would God save you and not my daughter too?" I sympathize with this family and grieve with them in the depth of their sorrow. What a heartbreaking question. Some believe they are special and surely the "one" God dearly loves, while others believe God does not love them at all. In contrast, Adina often jokingly refers to herself as "Daddy's favorite." Even the Apostle John referred to himself on several occasions as *the one Jesus loved*.[75] What we must know about the character of God is that He loves us all! Basically, there are no words we can share with someone who is grieving that will truly help them understand or console them during times of great heartache. We can only refer to the Word that tells us, He gives us "peace that surpasses all understanding" (Philippians 4:7). Scripture can validate what you are going through, it also helps you cope. Here is a Bible verse which conveys God's healing power in Adina's life:

> I, *the Lord God*, have seen *her* ways, but I will heal *her*; I will lead *her* and restore comfort to *her* and *her* mourners.
>
> *Isaiah 57:18, ESV (Modified for emphasis)*

A Mystery Revealed

Adina will be embarrassed by my description of her. I can hear her saying, "It's too much! It's all too much!" Our friendship goes way back. I first saw Adina in 1992. We worked together at the now defunct Tucson Cablevision. When I joined staff, she was a customer

---

[75] *John 13:23, John 21:7,* and *John 21:20.*

service representative. That first glimpse was unforgettable. Like a queen out of place, her head titled back and nose ever so slightly in the air, Adina arrived late. She walked into the service room crowded with rows of small cheerless gray cubicles, each hosting one swivel chair. Every head turned to watch her slide across the floor and take a seat at her desk. She was a stand-out in a room with roughly thirty other operators. Stunning, tall, easy to laugh and bossy, she made quite an impression and clearly captured the attention and support of what appeared to be a tiny tribe of followers. She was able to forge strong bonds with a variety of her co-workers, which seemed out of sorts in the dog-eat-dog work place. But her influence was concrete, and although I did not understand how she left such a powerful impression, my memory was indelibly marked.

After leaving the cable company, it would be many years before I would see Adina again. But as expected, when walking into the sanctuary at Grace Chapel (the name of the church at the time), she immediately caught my eye as she still commanded attention. She hugged me and smiled. "Hey Girl, It's so good to see you." Later while discussing her salvation story, she scolded me for not inviting her to church. I laughed because I tried, oh how I tried! Back in the 1990s, Adina did not readily embrace the message of Jesus as the *"truth and the life."*[xxx] Her views and spiritual journey eventually brought her to a life-changing revelation which passed any limited vision of her future. Exceeding the growth and development of other new converts, she was living and serving and speaking about God with a maturity that belied her youth in Christ. She found new niches to imbed her influences and sought opportunities to learn more, grow more, heal, and most of all sought places to serve the pastoral leadership and the people of God. In pursuit of all things Jesus, she offered her services to the pastor whom she petitioned to teach and mentor her in spiritual things. In hopes of scaring her off, Pastor Rae gave her a list of grunt duties to perform. But Adina never faltered. She embraced the dishes, laundry, babysitting and housework tasks without hesitation. She ran errands and typed letters, all while working at the side of a very busy spiritual visionary. Pastor Rae admits, "I never thought she would stick around."

What many saw in a less than ideal light, crediting Adina with a hidden agenda, Adina saw as putting her hand to the plow *(Luke 9:62)*. Her servant heart opened doors in ways that only living a righteous life could, and God was able to use her. I saw Adina growing. Grace walls were not high enough to keep her engaged. She joined citywide prayer groups, and attended prayer meetings in Tucson and Phoenix. By doing so, she found other godly women to mentor, guide, and teach her how to live a Christian life and become a *Proverbs 31* woman. Relentless in her passionate pursuits, she was not satisfied with a watered down, compromised, backseat view of serving the Lord, but rather pursued a sold-out, no holds barred, give it all to the Kingdom of God **race**. Unlike others who take years to achieve the same level of faith and trust, Adina rose to spiritual heights that seemed impossible in so short a time. She was working in *Kairos*[76] time. She continued to press in just like the **Word** instructs us to do:

> "I press on toward the goal for the prize of the upward call of God in Christ Jesus."
>
> *Philippians 3:14, (ESV)*

I believe what made her different from so many others engaging in the treadmill to ministry stardom was her crazy emphatic love for the Lord. Once I called to invite her out:

> "Hey Girl, how 'bout joining me for a chick flick, popcorn and some girl time?"

---

[76] *Kairos* is an ancient Greek word for time which refers to "the right or opportune moment."

"No can do!" she said. "It's date night."

"Date night! Adina, who are you datin'?"

I knew Adina had no time for a relationship, nor had she expressed interest in anyone, but her comment caught me off guard. It was Friday night and she had committed to spend time with the Lord in prayer. Confused, I asked for clarification. After work, she was going home to take a shower, curl her hair, put on a pretty dress, high heeled shoes, powder her nose, gloss her lips, and stroke mascara on each lash. Not forgetting the perfume, she crawled into her prayer closet (which literally meant the closet), and spent hours communing in fellowship with God. No other distractions, excuses or invitations tempted her.

> "When I was in the world, I used to do all that and more before going to bars to meet strangers who I had no love or interest in. How much more should I do to spend time with my God, the Lover of my soul?" she declared.

> I asked, "Isn't that a little radical?"

> "If you were gonna' present yourself before a king, wouldn't you prepare?" she asked.

> "Well, yeah!"

> "Okay then! I'm going before the Lord of lords and the King of kings, the one who loved me and saved me when I was unlovely, and un-loveable."

Amazed at the maturity and depth of passion she had for the Lord, this relatively new convert had achieved what so many

Christians, old and new alike, never do. She understood Jesus' death meant more than mere suffering. His crucifixion on Golgotha's Hill, the place of the Skull, meant redemption, restoration, wholeness purchased at the cost of everything, but so worth the relationship God seeks to have with each one of us. Her desire to worship, to seek His face, her love demonstrated in tears and time, were priceless sacrifices, that I believe, earned her great favor with God and man *(Luke 2:52).* [77]

I am not the only one who sees her character. She is nearly everyone's friend and carries such a prayer burden for those whom she loves. There are other people, those closest to her, who have their own peculiar stories. Co-worker and friend, Pastor Carol Torres says Adina "was a cohort who worked alongside me to advance the gospel message to a world in need." They pastored together at GTTN for about four years,[78] where Adina worked as the Youth Pastor. But she also noted she was radically saved and lifted out of a life of chaos and self-destruction. Further she adds, "Adina is a woman of prayer, a passionate warrior who pursues the presence of God and one who is also a dynamic evangelist. Her persona and messages are engaging and inspiring, and she operates for God under a Deborah-style anointing." And finally she added, "Adina will shamelessly exploit every opportunity to share the good news about Jesus. She is a trophy of God's power and grace." Her husband Trevor also speaks of his first impressions:

> I met Adina at a prayer meeting one night in 2006. We both have different interpretations of when we met, but one thing holds true – I was captivated. I was just coming back to the Lord and spent almost all of my free time in prayer and studying

---

[77] The word "man" in this reference refers to all mankind (male and female).

[78] Accurate as of the writing of this book.

the Bible. I didn't have time for distractions, but it seemed everywhere I went, she was there. We went to conferences, prayer meetings, and Bible studies. Once we went up to Phoenix to a friend's church to attend an all-night prayer vigil on New Year's Eve. Together with Matteo Guyro, another dear friend of ours, we took turns reading the *Word* out loud. We drove two hours to spend an hour interceding for God's spiritual blessings. We were crazy for the Lord, and as much as I tried to deny it, I was crazy about her.

There were a lot of challenges and obstacles along the way. We are from very different backgrounds. It seemed that almost everything about "us" made no sense at all, except one: we both loved Jesus and had a heart and passion for His kingdom and His people. With much prayer and fasting, I asked, and Adina agreed, to be my wife. We were married on August 7th, 2009. Adina and I have been through a lot and have seen God move and do some pretty amazing things.

Adina has many friends and moves influentially like few others. I could not believe the nearly miraculous growth that took place in her life and how quickly it all happened. I joined her supporters while watching godly character unfold. Having been able to witness her advance in the things of God with authority and power, I had to know how this was possible in someone so new to heavenly things and Christian kingdom business. Writing this book has shown me the depths of Adina's love and commitment. I have seen her spirit-man rise up while being humbled by the circumstances of the tragedy. Most impressive was her reaction when we began to work on the book's manuscript. During sessions Adina would pace the floor while I sat at the computer and typed her recounted memories. Appearing haunted by visualizations and imagery while laboring to describe her experience, she often clenched fists to her chest and swallowed tears planting her face in her palms as she wept.

Adina tried to explain how aware of her flesh she became before she left heaven. She voiced discovery of her sinful nature, something she kept referring to as her "earth-suit." I believe this knowledge is critical for the Christian and the non-believer alike. We are all wearing the same earth-suit, but we need revelation of what it means to wear God's protective armor.[79] As she shared her pain, Adina's facial expressions demonstrated the visualization of the spiritual battle between heaven and hell. What had my friend experienced? What kind of skirmish played out in her mind as she tried to make sense of her troubles? What was witnessed seemed to suggest a representation of flesh versus the spirit. But she fought her way through this nightmare separating what seemed like dream segments from hellish revelations. This journey led her to the foot of the cross where we all learn who we are versus who we can become in Jesus Christ.

Sure Adina has her own personal faults. No one is perfect, right? *"No one is righteous, no not one!"(Romans 3:10)*. I am not blind to Adina's humanity either. She has not lived a perfect life and her past is a record that contradicts great character transformation done during the last decade. I am not trying to build her up as if she is some kind of paragon or ideal; no, that would be like worshiping an idol. But I do want to put my observations into perspective. She has something special! As Adina would say, "Even Ray Charles can see that!" It seems necessary to point out there is only ONE inspiration who can be an example of righteousness for us and that is Jesus! Like

---

[79] See *Ephesians 6:11-13*.

Cynthia Ogden in heaven, "We always take a back seat to Him."[80] We must give God the glory, for He alone is worthy!

I suppose what makes Adina such a stand-out is the simple fact "She <u>loves</u> people!" It has been said, "…people from every walk of life feel and see her love and are drawn to her because of it. What they see is Jesus' Spirit living in her."

> Beloved, let us love one another, for love is of God; and everyone who loves is born of God and knows God….God is love, and he who abides in love abides in God, and God in him….And this commandment we have from Him: that he who loves God must love his brother also. *(1 John 4:7, 16b, and 21, NKJV).*

Proofs

And finally one of the most miraculous aspects of this story is its validity. In an age of counterfeit money, fake sugar, artificial joints, and plastic hair, there is always the imitation, manipulation and potential scam that will confuse, distort and misrepresent God and His purposes in the world. So we now address the validity, truth, and authenticity of what has been chronicled in this book. Surely the day will come when the truth of what Adina has shared will be challenged by those looking to discredit all that transpired. In addition to the story, its miraculous details, and the many witnesses, we offer this list of supplementary proofs as a record that what happened was real and reported to the best of each of the interviewees' and this writer's abilities. For those who doubt, you may pursue substantiation of the story through these provable indicators:

---

[80] Adina noted this about Cynthia during her recount of heaven in Chapter Ten.

- One of the first remaining proofs exists in the **911 *Call*** which was logged and recorded.

- Next while in the Green Room at Grace, Adina's phone randomly called Claire's grandfather without provocation. The entire field rescue effort of the EMTs was recorded during the emergency team's response. This call has been heard by many witnesses and can be reviewed by making a request to listen to the soundtrack. Immediately after the 911 call, Adina's phone, presumed in sleep mode--without anyone's direct assistance, dialed Claire's grandfather, Rubin N, Ph.D., (well-known psychologist and professor, specializing in dream and sleep medicine). He did not answer. The call went straight to voicemail. As EMT's rushed into the church, all rescue efforts were recorded and preserved for posterity on the phone.

- There are many eye witness reports from medical professionals, friends, family, and church members who all have a story to tell and observed some portion of Adina's tale. Scripture says speak to witnesses to validate something's veracity:

  > "A matter must be established by the testimony of two or three witnesses."
  >
  > *Deuteronomy 19:15, (NIV)*

- One of the most compelling proofs involves brain images denoting two *holes* in Adina's brain. Trevor recalls a doctor's visit where they looked at images of the brain and could clearly see two apparent holes. The doctor turned to Adina and said, "This picture compared to this woman makes no sense at all." Based on MRI results, he literally confirmed it was impossible, implying Adina should not be operating normally.

- Another proof is her story told in pictures. The MRI images of the injury indicate an apparent "milky film" etched across the brain. Doctors told Trevor not to have much hope and to expect her to be permanently damaged. The magnetic resonance images (MRI) of her brain say one thing, but her recovery proves something else. And of course, there are photographs of the hospital itself, some contained in this book.

- A recording was done by Cynthia Ogden's father (Mitch) who came to visit Adina days after being released from the hospital. Using a hand recorder, he made a disk of her recollections of the heaven experience.

- One of the greatest proofs, especially personal to me, involves efforts to write this book. The fact remains within weeks of Adina's release from the hospital; we began working on the manuscript. The composition phase from beginning to end took over five years. Adina, Trevor and I began working to outline the content on March 19, 2012. The first chapter written was, of course, the heaven piece. This was done to ensure time would not alter the memories and that we could capture every thought or event before the images had opportunity to fade. As time went on, I realized how critically important this was. During collaboration, it seemed Adina's anointing had a Moses-like-glow[xxxi] and what she had to say at the time was most significant. It was so important to put it down before age altered the memory or time ruined what we felt the Spirit wanted to record.

- The amazing prayer response of people worldwide is a proof and a miracle. There is not much more to add regarding this issue as it was addressed in Chapter 8.

- One of the more peculiar proofs is in the thirteen day timeline of Adina's recovery in the ICU. She entered the hospital on Sunday, February 5th, and was discharged on Friday, February 17th. In the following chart it is broken down to make visually apparent how miraculous her medical restoration really was:

Date	Day of Week	Days in Hospital	Details
Feb. 5	Sunday	1st Day	Day of incident: Reparative surgery. Iced body to preserve tissue and organ function and two blood transfusions. [Adina was unresponsive from February 7–10, the period referred to as the *coma* state].
Feb. 8	Wednesday	4th Day	Began returning body to normal temperature.
Feb. 9	Thursday	5th Day	Body reached normal temperature goals.
Feb. 10	Friday	6th Day	The first day she opened her eyes.
Feb. 11	Saturday	7th Day	Adina showed cognition for the first time.
Feb. 12	Sunday	8th Day	Adina gained cognitive consciousness.
Feb. 13	Monday	9th Day	First day she was able to write her responses on a tablet.
Feb. 14	Tuesday	10th Day	Valentine's Day.
Feb. 15	Wednesday	11th Day	Tracheal tube was removed.
Feb. 16	Thursday	12th Day	Adina walked around the ICU with a walker.
Feb. 17	Friday	13th Day	Moved out of ICU to patient room. Two hours later was discharged from hospital.

- An obvious physical proof is the fact Adina is standing, functioning, living and has returned to her normal life prior to the incident. Even doctors agree her recovery was nothing short of miraculous, and she is the greatest evidence of all.

- The final tangible proof is the record of her story as found in this book. The story is not a fabrication, fantasy or fiction. It is real and has been reported as accurately and with as much integrity as this reporter could possibly muster to meet the challenge of allowing the Holy Spirit to tell His story.

And here we have tried to tell God's story. We give Him all the glory!

Epilogue

But I am like a green olive tree[81] in the house of God;
I trust in the mercy of God forever and ever.
Psalm 52:8 (NKJV)

Return to Normal Life

Upon release, in between moments of sharing my story, which I did with everyone, and the quiet times I spent in shock trying to process it all, I was struggling. Breathing, walking, and seeing were no longer normal functions I took for granted. My depth perception was askew, and I missed a few tables while leaning against them for balance. Getting to the bathroom and using the facilities were no longer simple tasks either. My dear husband was tethered with these perfunctory things and performed them all with such sacrifice and tenderness. Wheeling out the hospital doors, I was still very weakened by muscle deterioration. Trevor and I were excited to be going home, and a bit apprehensive as to what the future held. We knew God's word concerning healing, but just because *you know where the journey ends* does not mean you know how to get there or what it might look like. We struggled with all sorts of doubts.

---

[81] Olive trees are long living plants, and can grow to be quite large, but they are one of the only trees that are <u>hallow</u>! Like the olive tree, we must fill ourselves with God's Spirit and not the things of the world. *1 Corinthians 1:27-31 (NIV)*.

Returning to normal life was not so easy either. This became evident while at a friend's house one lazy Monday afternoon. After some goodies, two loads of dirty drawers, socks, t-shirts, and a glass of iced coffee, I picked up my laundry basket full of freshly folded clothes and began to carry my burden to the car. While trying to pick up my right leg to make the next step in what nearly everyone takes for granted and have done since the age of two, I had what I can only describe as a "brain disconnect." My brain sent the message to my leg, but my leg received no impulse, proof the body follows where the brain leads. My leg did not move. I could feel myself falling, but was helpless to control or stop the inevitable crash. "Adina, let go of the basket."

Unable to comply, my body was in motion and all I could do was hang on for the ride and laugh about it afterwards. My body slammed full force to the ground, not just once but several times as I first hit the pavement landing on my knee, then scooted forward as the basket seemed to drag me into a prostrate position. Thankfully, the laundry load cushioned my fall. Nowadays, these kinds of quirky random movements are not uncommon, but praise God, they diminish daily. I pray my brain disconnects are a short-term consequence, soon to be a distant part of the incident aftermath. I needed and am receiving special progressive treatment to completely restore all facets of my brain to full function. I praise God as this is another of the continuing miracles I still see unfolding! Trevor explains more:

> There were two holes in the base of her brain which affected her nervous system and motor skills. As the Lord has directed us to pray, the holes have begun to shrink, and to date one has healed completely. In prayer, the Lord revealed she would be completely healed, and then some. Not sure exactly what that means, but He confirmed His word many times

over, so that is what we continue to believe. We are still praying a total and complete healing. But with the exception of the scar on her neck, you would never know anything happened.

I have to mention this work of a special physician who will remain anonymous. Specializing in recovery of brain injuries, I met him in the latter part of 2013, through a referral from Robby Booth. The cost for his therapy runs in the thousands. Without disclosing the kindness of others, I give the glory to the Lord, for the financing was miraculously made available. And my therapy continues to make strides towards a whole, restored, neural network. Thank you Jesus for fixing what seemed impossible.

What I learned during this prolonged process and through the guidance of this earthly angel was we desire to be whole and to make sure our *T's* are crossed and the *I's* are dotted. When this doctor said there were residual holes in my brain caused by the trauma and all I had been through, I reminded him Jesus had holes too. But the holes in Jesus' hands did not stop Him from doing the work He was resurrected to do. And I added, I would not let this situation hinder me either. I believed then, as I still do, we all have work to do and no matter what may limit us, we are supposed to press on to complete what God has required of us. Once believers recognize this for themselves, the miraculous works we will achieve are limitless.

What is impossible with men is possible with God (*Luke 18:27, ESV*).

Update

At the time of this writing it has been roughly five years since we said goodbye to hospital gowns, and what Trevor calls, "the cafeteria's glorious Philly cheese steaks." I continue to recover as God gives us guidance, direction and wisdom. It has been a wrestling-match dealing with appointments, medications, medical bills, as well as the physical therapy and neuro-tremors that stem from the anoxic brain injury. I have gone from wheelchair to walker to heels.

My family and I have grown a lot too. God could have just healed me, but instead He has broken and multiplied me, and as a result healed something in all of us. He truly has walked with us through this valley and our faith is so much greater because of it. We know Him as comforter, healer, warrior, reconciler, intercessor, and friend. This process has taken us from a place where people begged for a temporary miracle in a time of desperation, to pursuing the process of long term self-replicating miracles that expand His Kingdom and transfer eternal value. "Surrounded by family, friends and ministry partners, many of whom stayed with us almost the entire time, my recovery truly was a group effort as His people came together in one accord to seek His face on my behalf. It was a humbling experience, I believe, for us all," Trevor said.

In 2007, I gave my life to Jesus. I came from a background that did not miss opportunities to do those things which make God sad.[xxxii] But His plan of restoration for my life was definite. Once I decided to completely surrender myself to the Lord, I did so with ridiculous abandonment. Anyone who knew me before saw a radical change in my way of thinking and how I lived. I remember being in prayer several months following the day I was born again, July 7, 2007 (the real moment I rooted myself in the things of God). At the time I said, "I'm never going back!" I had a salvation experience years before, but I was really just playing games. I was not immersed. At that moment, I married the Lord, a permanent decision I have never regretted. I even have the date "7.7.7" tattooed on my arm as a reminder, a symbol of my undying love for my Savior.

My Tree

Since dedicating my life, God often speaks to me with the most impressive revelations during prayer. And what makes this event so remarkable is He showed me a vision several weeks before the actual day of the incident. During that prayer time, I spoke with the *Author and Finisher of our faith*,[82] and felt the Lord grab my attention by covering me with a blanket of warm safety, hemming me in with His love. As I lay there, enjoying His presence, He brought me back to a special place, a memory of my past long since forgotten.

The Lord spoke and said, "I've always known you."

I was thinking in my mind. "Well, where were you? Remember the trauma in my childhood? I can't believe you were there?"

"Yes, I was there," He said.

He began to show me in those dark nights when I was being abused, places where I could have lost my life. He was there! From the beginning of my childhood helping me endure maltreatment, He was pressing in to let me know this lifestyle was not for me. His grace covered every situation until I came to the place where I could say, "He is real!" I often thought my personal insights were due to my own intuition, thinking I was my own god. But the Lord showed me it was His influence in my life all along. After revealing the images of where I had been, He took me back even further to the day under the tree in upstate New York. Once again, I saw the crimson leaves, creamy yellow vegetation and burnt orange foliage. The solace provided by my giant oak tree loomed large in my mind's eye.

"Do you remember when you were a little girl underneath your much-loved tree and you saw the light dancing through the autumn leaves?"

---

[82] Hebrew 12:2

There it was again, my old friend with sunlight
coming through the branches, but this time, I saw
the sunrise. As soon as He mentioned the dancing
light skipping in the tree, the memory came in like
a flood. I was undone. I remembered as a child
asking, "Is that You, God? Is that You?"

As soon as I heard his voice ask if I remembered the tree, it was
as if He brought me right back to that moment in time, that memory
of the oak tree and the incredible dancing light. I could visualize
the whole day, the place and the moment when He assured me I
was not alone.

"It WAS You! You were there, Lord."

I always thought I was alone, but then I knew He had always
been there and always loved me. I remembered His presence in my
past even in the *tiniest*[83] details. I think the Lord was guaranteeing
His placement in life's circumstances by reminding me of the tree
prior to the accident. He wanted me to know that He is always with
me! I think He prepared me for what was to come. I had to know
He would keep me safe and never leave my side to be able to face this
scary journey with confidence and hope. Although I did not know
about the coming tragedy, I trusted the Lord's care for me! Now I
see it as Him lighting the way and providing continual comforting
remembrances of "the tree" as I was in recovery. It makes me smile
remembering the tree outside my hospital window.

Like my childhood revelation, the Lord is always speaking to
each individual in a unique and special way, something that is
personal and relates to them. I am sure if you think for a moment
you too have had similar revelations, little reminders; a symbol or
image that prompts you to recall who you are and who He is to

---

[83] Means tiny, smallest, minuscule.

you! I encourage you to take that memory in prayer to the Father and ask Him to reveal himself, His love for you, and (if you have not already accepted Him as your Savior), receive His salvation plan for your life. I would be remiss as a servant of the Lord if I did not offer every reader, who has not already prayed the sinner's prayer, a chance to do so:

> **Dear Lord Jesus,**
>
> **I know I am a sinner, and I ask for your forgiveness. I believe you died for my sins and rose from the dead. I trust and follow you as my Lord and Savior. Guide my life and help me to do your will, so I may eventually join you in heaven.**
>
> **In your name Jesus,**
>
> **Amen.**

Final Thoughts

As previously mentioned, the Lord gave me two messages while in heaven. The story of "The Machine" was for all believers, but He also had a personal and special message just for me. He told me I had to go back to my life on earth.

> I could not stay in heaven because, "You have babies to raise," He said.
>
> At first I thought, "I only have Claire."

Frankly, I never desired to work with kids. In fact, that would have been my invitation to walk out the door. But in due time I realized the revelation was about spiritual babies, those just coming into the church, and the youth joining God's ranks. Now there is nothing I would rather do than love on those God has entrusted to me. Each new "reborn"[84] is another form of baby…babes in Christ; all kinds of believers at different levels of growth and maturity. These babies are my spiritual fruit. Within nine months (the time it takes a baby to form in the mother's womb) of returning to work, I was asked to become the pastor for a youth group of roughly 10 to 15 young people. Two months later we had 75 weekly attenders at our regular meetings.

The hardest part about mentoring babies is walking with them and staying through the good, the bad and the ugly until they are in a place where they stand on their own. In other words, we are called to discipleship. We as leaders and "disciple-ers" must be the emissaries of hope for children, our families, and the future. A mature Christian who will stay and walk by the side of a newborn is fulfilling all that God would have them do. In these times, new believers (aka babes in Christ) do not trust, because so many others have let them down. You have to stay and show them you will walk with them and are there for them. It is not easy, but it is necessary!

Before the final word, first I want Trevor, the head of our household to share his thoughts on behalf of our family:

> This has been a prayerfully-charged journey that is still unfolding. We thank God, our friends and family, our church and pastors, and all of the people around the globe who stood and are still standing in the gap for us. Thank you.

Finally, this book has brought me to one primary truth. I want to love God; I mean really love Him, which means living out His commands no matter the cost. And it is the job of every Christian

---

[84] *John 3:3* and *John 3:7.*

to teach others to do the same. I plan to live every day of what is left of my life as if it could be my last (because it could!).

Because of God's great love, I truly do **know** by His grace the Savior waits for me beyond the grave. And to that, I only add one last thought, "I must let go of heaven or run the risk of never being able to accomplish what God wants me to do here on earth!"

> [Jesus] was taken up before their very eyes, and a cloud hid him from their sight. The [disciples] were looking intently up into the sky as he was going, when suddenly two men dressed in white stood beside them. "Men of Galilee," they said, "why do you stand here looking into the sky? This same Jesus, who has been taken from you into heaven, will come back in the same way you have seen him go into heaven" *(Acts 1:9-11, NIV)*.

In other words, "Get to work!"

Glossary

Analogy: is a similarity between two things, which is used to create a comparison.

Anaphylaxis: is a serious allergic reaction known for a rapid onset of symptoms which can cause death in reportedly 5% of the cases (roughly one out of every twenty incidents).

Anoxic: Medical term meaning an abnormally low amount of oxygen in the body tissues, often referred to as "hypoxia."

Apostle: the word means "to be sent." Traditional definition of apostle is any of the original 12 disciples called by Jesus to preach the gospel that were sent out to spread the Good News.

Apparatus: instruments, machinery, tools, or materials, with a specific function.

Apprehensive: means to be fearful about something terrible that could potentially happen.

Arctic Sun Protocol: a system involving chemically induced paralysis and a cooling procedure used in emergency care situations to save lives.

Aura: means "subtly pervasive quality or atmosphere seen as emanating from a person, place, or thing" per the online dictionary: *http://dictionary.reference.com/browse/aura?s=t;* and it is not to be confused with the term which refers to *auras* as they relate to the occult.

Baruch Sheamar: The first blessing of Pesukei Dezimra. Pesukei Dezimra is a group of praises, psalms, verses or blessings spoken during daily Jewish morning services.

Benadryl: is a popular brand of antihistamine used to treat simple allergy symptoms like sneezing, runny nose, itchy and watery eyes.

BFF: an abbreviation for the phrase, "best friends forever."

Blind Man's Bluff: a form of tag, where the person who is "it" is blind-folded.

Body Cooling Procedure: this medical procedure slows down metabolism and allows the body time to heal itself. Body cooling to 33 degrees Celsius or 91.4 degrees Fahrenheit is ideal per medical procedure by neurosurgeons at San Francisco General Hospital Medical Center.

Bride of Christ: this phrase references the church, which Jesus gave His life for, died for, and will again come for per scripture references in *Ephesians 5:25-27, Revelations 21:2, Revelations 21:9, and John 14:3,* respectively.

Cacophony: dissonance; or a meaningless fusion of sounds that do not naturally blend well.

Cardiopulmonary Arrest: means the patient's heart has stopped working.

Capricious: meaning unpredictable or changing.

CEO: is an abbreviation for *Chief Executive Officer,* otherwise known as the head of a large organization, who usually holds the highest position in the company.

Challah bread: Is a double loaf of bread commemorating manna that fell from heaven when the Israelites wandered in the desert for forty years following the Exodus from Egypt *(Numbers 32:13)*. Each single loaf is sometimes woven with six strands. Together, both loaves represent the tribes of Israel. Other numbers of strands are also commonly used: three, five and seven.

Chameleon: is easily changeable.

Charades: a game where teams take turns to act out words, phrases, titles or events using pantomime to help teammates guess the clue.

Christian: means to be Christ-like.

Christianese: is a made-up term used to describe religion-based specific terms, concepts and ideals common to the Christian community.

Churchy: a made up word to indicate overly religious and legalistic behavior often associated with Christians.

Cliff Hanger: is a an adventure ending in suspense aimed at engaging viewer in next event.

Coded: is a slang term doctors use to explain a ***cardiopulmonary arrest*** event requiring immediate resuscitation. It means the patient's heart has stopped.

Coincidence: an occurrence of simultaneous events that appears to be occurring by mere chance, or a deliberate sign of God's intervention in our circumstances.

Colloquialisms: an informal, but relative use of mutual terms used in ordinary speech often indicative of a specific group who share commonalities.

Coma: caused or instigated by severe injury or illness, coma is a prolonged deep state of unconsciousness that can last indefinitely; or a condition which can be induced purposely using prescribed chemicals called, "induced coma."

Concrete: meaning for this text is "to be real."

Consigned: meaning committed.

Corporeal: means to be tangible or of a physical nature.

Corrosive elements: An erosive component that destroys other contacted substances.

CPR: is an abbreviation for *cardiopulmonary resuscitation*, which is a medical procedure involving repeated compression of chest to restore heart activity, blood circulation and breathing of someone whose heart stopped.

Crib: Slang term for home, domicile, or dwelling.

Cricothyro: Slang term for home, domicile, or dwelling

Crucifixion: an ancient form of punishment and death that involved being nailed to a cross or tree at the hands/wrists and feet. This form of torture was death by asphyxiation. With victim's arms extended the lungs would be fully expanded, unable to breathe properly, and ultimately would fill with fluid. In order to gasp for air, pulling up on the nails in the wrists and feet would cause additional pain. Death could take hours or days for individual to expire. In addition to his beating, whipping and humiliation, Jesus was crucified at 9:00 a.m., *(Mark 15:24-25, Mark 15:27)* and died 6 hours later at 3:00 p.m., *(Mark 15:34-37,* and *Matthew 27:49-54).*

David's Mighty Men: refers to 37 men who formed a type of Special Forces army that was particularly close to King David of the Bible. There are roughly 71 references to "Mighty Men" in KJV scripture with references that run from Genesis to Revelations. This text refers to *1 Chronicles 11:10-13.*

Death: is defined as the *permanent* cessation of all essential functions of the body including the heartbeat, brain activity and breathing.

Deploy: to move strategically or fittingly; or to make ready for use by coming into a position.

Diagnosis: the scientific analysis by which one classifies the characteristics and circumstances of any medical condition resulting in a decision about the illness/disease based on examination. This process precedes prognosis.

Direction of Care: when emergency personnel transport patients to hospital emergency rooms during medical crises, they must hand the patient over to the care of a doctor. They are not allowed to merely deliver someone without transferring their care to a qualified medical professional. See also: *Transfer of Custody.*

Disciple(s): means one is a *disciplined learner* and/or a follower of Jesus Christ.

Dr. Cynthia Ogden: [Obituary] OGDEN, Cynthia R, MD, went to be with the Lord on May 9, 2011 at the age of 47. Cynthia grew up in the greater Portland, Oregon area. She attended Portland State University and medical school at the Oregon Health Science University. She is survived by her loving family: parents, Milt and Karolyn Ogden; brothers, David and Randy; sister, Stephanie; nephews, Geoffrey, Stephen, Joshua, Michael, Nathaniel, Zachary and nieces, Rebecca, Emily and Anna Grace as well as many dear friends in the medical community and her church families in San Carlos and Tucson. Memorial Service will be held at Grace to the Nations Church, Tucson, Saturday, May 14, 2011, 2:30 p.m. In lieu of flowers, donations to Grace to the Nations Benevolence Fund are appreciated. *Published in the Arizona Daily Star on May 11, 2011.*

Dr. Fredy T, General Internist: for the sake of this text, Dr. Fredy was not directly interviewed. All quotes accredited to him were a result of third party interviews.

Dr. McDreamy: is a comic reference and play on words to the fictional surgeon Dr. Derek Shepherd on the medical drama *Grey's Anatomy.* This character is portrayed by actor Patrick Dempsey who is lovingly referred to by fans as Dr. McDreamy because of his amazing good looks.

Drawers: the Urban Dictionary says this a slang term used to describe women's knickers. It derives its meaning most likely from the reference to dresser drawers where underwear is kept.

Drug Induced Coma: Derived from the Greek word *"koma"* the online medical dictionary states the meaning of the word *coma* is a "deep sleep" marked by unresponsiveness even to painful stimuli, accompanied by loss of normal reflexes.

Drug-induced State: another way to say drug induced coma.

Dyspneic: difficulty breathing.

Earmark: an identifying or characteristic marker that suggests something special has been set aside for a particular purpose.

Earth-suit: this is a term coined by Adina to describe what it felt like to shed her sinful earthly flesh, which she compared to body armor or a suit of clothing for covering the body.

Ebonics: Is considered an English dialect by some and American black English by others who regard it as a language in its own right.

EKG: is an abbreviation for the term "electrocardiogram." An EKG is a test designed to check for problems with electric heart activity.

Elders: the church's spiritual leaders, shepherds of the body at Grace to the Nations.

Elite: the choicest or the best of something.

Emissaries: someone sent on a mission to represent the message of the sender.

EMT: an abbreviation for Emergency Medical Technician.

Enemy of Our Soul: is another *identifier* or name for Satan.

ENT: stands for Ear, Nose, & Throat, and usually referring to a specialized physician.

Enterprise: a project or undertaking, specifically one that is important or difficult requiring boldness or great effort.

Epi: is a slang term for EpiPen, a medical device used to dispense epinephrine through an auto-injector in measured doses. Dispensing this chemical narrows blood vessels and opens lung airways, to diminish allergic symptoms.

ER: is an abbreviation referring to Emergency Room.

Essence: the basic nature or qualities of a thing that make it unique.

Evangelism/Evangelist: preaching the gospel to convert the lost; and zealous performance of missionary activities.

Evil: is the absence of good, like darkness is the absence of light.

Exsanguinate: to drain of blood or make bloodless; to bleed to death.

Façade: a superficial or decorative front giving an illusion or false appearance.

Facets: one of many aspects, features, traits or characteristics of something.

Fasting: can be times of testing or temptation. See Jesus's Temptation in the Desert in *Mark 1:13*. The purpose of fasting is to deny yourself pleasure in order to dedicate yourself to seeking the Lord, praying, studying the Word and listening for His direction for your life. Fasting is like hitting pause on your life, removing all outside distractions so you can commune with God in prayer. For many, *fasting* means skipping meals, eating s specific diet or cutting out fatty or sugary foods to cleanse the body and the mind.

Global Brain Damage: a layman's term for the medical name, *"global cerebral ischemia"* describing the result of insufficient blood flow to the brain which leads to death of brain tissue, which is usually triggered by cardiac arrest. Injury manifests with impairment to vision or blindness, body movement, coordination and weakness, and can affect speech. Poor blood flow for more than ten seconds results in unconsciousness, and for more than a few minutes generally produces irreversible brain damage.

Golgotha's Hill: Jesus was crucified on Calvary, also called Golgotha's Hill, the place of the Skull because the rouged, rocky location appeared to form the image of a skull visible from certain angles in the hillside.

Good News: is another way to say "the Gospel," which is the message about salvation that Jesus died and rose again for our sins *(Romans 8:34, NLT)*, and if we accept His sacrifice *(1 John 1:9)*, we are reconciled with our Heavenly Father *(Romans 5:10)*.

Gracers: is a made-up name used to describe members or attendees of Grace to the Nations church in Tucson, Arizona.

Gray Zone: is *med speak* for any area of patient care which the parameters of good practice are not clearly defined, neither are they black or 'white. May also be called a "gray area."

GTTN: an abbreviation for Grace to the Nations.

HaMotzi: Shabbat blessings over the bread before a meal.

Hell: there are many descriptions and speculations of what and where hell is located, who goes there and who does not. Scripture mentions it roughly 54 times according to the King James Version of the Bible. Hell is a place without God. Since God is love *(1 John 4:16)*, meaning not merely that He loves, gives love, or has love, but that He is **actually** LOVE, than we cannot know truly love without

Him. God is what love represents; He is love manifested physically. Therefore, hell is a place without all that He provides, represents and brings with His presence. In its simplest definition hell is "**the absence of God!**"

House prophet: a person who speaks for God by divine inspiration. At GTTN, someone recognized as a gifted prophet who is honored and respected within the ministry as called by God to encourage and strengthen the body of Christ.

Hypoxia: Medical term meaning an abnormally low amount of oxygen in the body tissues, often referred to as "anoxic."

Iced Coffee: a favorite drink of Adina's where one pours coffee over ice and cream.

ICU: is an acronym for Intensive Care Unit, a department in the hospital which provides critical care for seriously ill patients.

Intercession: is a type of prayer by an "intercessor" who prays, often pleading, to God on behalf of another person.

IV: is an abbreviation of the term "intravenous;" a tube used to delivery mediations, fluids, and nutrients to the body of a patient.

Juxtaposition: to compare or contrast something side by side.

Kabbalat Shabbat: is the name for receiving the Shabbat.

Kairos: is an ancient Greek word for time which refers to "the right or opportune moment." *Kairos* time is the spiritual opposite of *chronos* time. While mankind moves and operates in chronological events (a progression of ordered events), God moves in Kairos events (a moment of indeterminate time in which an event of significance happens, which is usually moving very quickly or in miraculous ways).

Kevin Bacon: "Six degrees of separation" is a popular theory fostering the idea everyone is only six steps away from anyone else on the planet. Through introduction everyone can be connected via a friend through a maximum of six others.

Kiddush: a blessing recited over a cup of wine and/or bread during festivals and on Sabbath.

Lazarus: In the Book of John, we learn of a friend of Jesus whom He raises from the dead named Lazarus. See *John 11:43 (KJV)*.

Longsuffering: Means: "enduring injury, trouble, or provocation long and patiently." So many like to say God is wrong because He is not tolerant. Well clearly He is not tolerant. He allowed evil men to kill His only son *(John 3:16)*. No, God is a loving Father who endures our negative behaviors because He loves us so much! He gives us every opportunity to repent and return to Him. He is waiting. He is longsuffering!

Manifest (or Manifested): to make clear or plainly understood.

Manna: Sweet honey-like bread miraculously supplied every day to the Israelites in the wilderness. They were to collect just enough to feed them and their families for one day *(Exodus 16:14–36)*.

Masquerade: a disguise or false outward appearance, mask, pretense or a façade.

Matrix: a place or point where something develops or emerges; can be a point of origin.

Matrix moment: refers to the 1999 science fiction movie, The Matrix, dealing with a post-apocalyptic society where the hero is able to slow down time and move through it hyper fast.

Med Speak: is a term conveying medical specific terms, language and colloquialisms specific to the industry.

Minutiae: a matter of precise details; something small or considered a trivial, petty matter.

Miracle Lady, The: a name given to Adina by hospital emergency room staff.

Miracles: extraordinary events which surpass all known powers and can only be ascribed to supernatural causes.

Moniker: is a fancy word for name or nickname.

MRI: Magnetic resonance imaging is a form of high-frequency measurement that records the atomic nuclei of body tissue and radio waves within a strong magnetic field. The result is a clear and detailed image of the body's internal organs.

MRSA: is an acronym for the term "Methicillin-resistant Staphylococcus aureus," an often hospital bound bacterium responsible for several difficult-to-treat human infections.

Neural Synapses: Loosely means nerve ending connections.

Nurse Ratchet: A fictional character from the 1962 novel and movie of the same name, "One Flew Over the Cuckoo's Nest," whose reputation was one of strict adherence to the establishment and unyielding order in a mental care environment.

Olive Trees: are known to live for very long periods of time. As they age, the trees grow quite large, and unlike other trees, the center core becomes hollow. Many theologians make reference to the tree being a kind of representation of Christian believers, who must fill their hollow nature with the Holy Spirit.

OR: is an abbreviation for the word *operating room*.

Otolaryngology: is a branch of medicine dealing with the anatomy, function, and diseases of the ear, nose, and throat.

Pavlov's Dog: refers to research and a series of experiments conducted by Physiologist Ivan Pavlov on his dog where he trained him to salivate (in anticipation of dinner) at the sound of a bell. Called conditional reflex (1901), this was done to demonstrate humans can be taught via classical conditioning. As it relates to this story, the possibility of learning about Adina's heaven experience created the same excitement and anticipation regarding details of her story.

Peeps: is street slang for the word "people." Also a recognized Ebonics term meaning the same thing.

Perioperative: *Peri* is a prefix which means around or about, and "perioperative" means procedure occurs during surgery.

Philly Cheese Steaks: A sandwich made with beef strips, caramelized onions, mushrooms, and sautéed peppers on a hoagie roll with melted provolone cheese and mustard.

Place of the Skull, Golgotha's Hill: also known as Cavalry, the location of Jesus' crucifixion.

Portrayal: to make a likeness or describe graphically.

Posterity: for future generations; to assure longevity.

Power of the Highest: another moniker for the Holy Spirit.

Prayer Warrior: individuals committed to pray. Their battlefield takes place in prayer.

Precipice: on the edge of a cliff or a situation of great peril.

Process: an operation or series of steps occurring in a particular manner.

Profane: meaning unconsecrated or irreligious, not devoted to holy purposes, characterized by irreverence or contempt for God, sacred things or concepts.

Progeny: meaning spiritual offspring.

Prognosis: Following diagnosis, experts predict disease outcomes, probable recovery plan(s), and design a course of action hopefully to aid in patient's restoration to wellness and/or return to normal health.

Prophecy: (noun) something declared by a prophet, especially a divinely inspired prediction, instruction, or exhortation given by the Spirit of God.

Prophesy: (verb) means to declare or predict by divine intervention.

Prostrate: to lay flat on the ground face down; to be reduced to helplessness or weakness, to be humbled.

Proverbial: likened to *proverbs* characteristic of a commonly known wisdom.

Purity: meaning nothing added.

Purview: the range of someone's vision or understanding.

Race: in this context, a contest or competition where getting to the finish line is the goal.

Ray Charles: was an American rhythm and blues singer, songwriter, musician, and composer who was blind from birth. But his disability did not hinder his genius or talent *(September 23, 1930-June 10, 2004).*

Reborn: as scripture denotes in *John 3:3,* you must be born again (meaning born of the spirit), which only relationship with God can do, or you cannot see heaven (aka: the Kingdom of God).

Restoration: the act of being renewed, restored, revived, or to be returned to an unimpaired state.

Resurrection: means to be raised from death to life. *Source, Merriam-Webster Online Dictionary: http://www.merriam-webster. com/dictionary/resurrection.*

Resuscitation: to bring someone who is unconscious, not breathing, or close to death back to a conscious or active state once again. *Source, Merriam-Webster Online Dictionary: http://www.merriam-webster.com/dictionary/resuscitation.*

Revered: meaning to regard with respect, honor, esteem or worship.

Righteousness: the quality of being just or a state of rightness. This is a highly debated subject among Christians in America. There are roughly 306 scripture references in the software version of KJV. Clearly it is biblically essential, but the standard which God calls us to and which He claims is blessed, is so often compromised. *1 Peter*

1:13-16 "Therefore gird up the loins of your mind, be sober, and rest your hope fully upon the grace that is to be brought to you at the revelation of Jesus Christ; as obedient children, not conforming yourselves to the former lusts, as in your ignorance; but as He who called you is holy, you also be holy in all your conduct, because it is written, 'Be holy, for I am holy'" *(NKJV)*.

Robby Booth: is a humble man who prefers to be known as "An ordinary guy serving an extraordinary God!" He has served the Foursquare Church as supervisor of the Pacific Region, Chaplains District supervisor, chairman of the National Camp Facilities Board and as a member of the Foursquare Cabinet. Formerly senior pastors of Faith Chapel Foursquare Church in Glendale, Ariz., for 11 years, and Robby was divisional superintendent over Central Arizona. The Booths later moved to Modesto, where Robby became supervisor of the historic Western District in 1995. Under his leadership, the district planted approximately 130 churches and developed ministry training institutes. Dual major bachelor's degree in Christian ministries and counseling from Hope University, followed by a master's degree in marriage and family counseling from Azusa Pacific University. He has presented marriage conferences across the U.S. and in Canada. *Source quoted from: http://www.foursquare.org/ news/article/foursquare_district_list_and_map_now_available#robby*

Rûach: (pronounced *roo-ahk)* is the Hebrew word meaning "Spirit, wind, breath of the mouth; to breathe out." Some scholars agree *rûach* can also mean "wind of heaven" and represents the creative breath of God.

Rûach Elohim: (pronounced *roo-ahk el-o-heem)* is the Hebrew word meaning "Spirit of God" hovering over the waters.

Sabbath: is a day set aside for rest and worship, and in modern times is usually recognized or celebrated as falling on Sunday. It is considered a *holy day.*

Salvation Story: refers to someone's testimony: events communicating their decision to accept Jesus as Savior.

Sapling: a young tree.

Saturated: for this text, completely soaked, drenched, inundated with a flood of emotion.

Saved: Being "saved" is a term mentioned 57 times in the KJV New Testament and 11 times by Jesus himself. Some basic verses that best convey this idea can be found in: *John 3:17, John 10:9, Mark 16:16, and Acts 2:21.* The concept of being saved means you are rescued from the coming wrath of God *(Romans 5:9-11).*

Scarlet deluge: an historic and literary way to refer to the flow of a lot of blood.

Secular: refers to the non-spiritual.

Segregate: to set apart from the main group, to isolate or individualize.

Self-Replicating: means to reproduce itself by some inherent power.

Sepulcher: meaning a place of burial.

Sequela: a morbid condition which occurs as a consequence of some catalytic event. As used in this case, the possibility of brain damage caused by of the lack of oxygen.

Shabbat: commemorates a day of rest honoring God who rested from creating the world. *Exodus 34:21* states, "Six days you shall work, but on the seventh day you shall rest" (NKJV). Shabbat is considered a day of peace and holiness.

Sista: *(pronounced "sis-tah").* *A* slang term for the word *sister* used to communicate the closest of friends *(Proverbs 18:24).* In **Ebonics** *"sista"* means a "strong black woman."

Slain in the Spirit: The term *"slain in the Spirit"* is used among Charismatic Christians to denote a spiritual movement on someone with such force they are overcome by the presence of the Holy Spirit, occasionally causing them to fall to the ground, and which can result in temporary unconsciousness.

Slice *or* Sliced: To cut through or cleave as if with a knife in to parts.

Soul Tie: reflects attachment in relationships beyond the normal closeness of friends. There are good and bad soul ties. Jonathan and David are said to have been linked in a way that made them value their friendship as much as their own lives, a good soul tie *(1Samuel 18:1, BBE).*

Sepulcher: a tomb, crypt or burial place.

Speaking Out: For the sake of this book, this phrase refers to the *prayers of the saints.* See *Acts 12:1-11* for more information.

Stand in the Gap: to stand in the gap means to place yourself where you are needed most for the benefit of others.

Stop, Drop and Roll: refers to the three fire safety steps taught to children and others in case of accidental fire; designed to minimize injury. In the text, it is used as an analogy for extreme circumstances comparing spiritual handling of challenging or difficult cases where someone is in danger of spiritual death.

Stuff: usually refers to property, equipment, things, and /or personal belongings. But can be anything that hinders you: the love of money, addiction, co-dependency, un-forgiveness, your car, your kids, your job, and anything that could separate you from God's purposes for your life.

Subglottic Stenosis: Although rare this condition is generally the result of a problematic airway intubation or a result of a life-threatening airway emergency.

Suffice: adequately meeting the need or purpose.

Supernatural: unexplainable and beyond normal, and intervention only attributable to God's almighty, unlimited authority, and infinite power.

Supplication: means to humbly pray, entreat, or petition God.

Tangible Proof: material, substantial and discernable evidence that something is real.

Teen Challenge: a drug rehabilitation program that works with men from teens to adulthood who struggle with substance abuse using a routine of healing Christ-centered initiatives.

Testimony: in Christian circles, testimony means sharing your own salvation story as evidence in support of a changed life; it is a factual statement of proof that declares Jesus is real. See *John 4:39.*

The Call: this phrase can refer to a number of Christian-themed concepts, events, or groups. For the most part the origin of "the

Call" refers to "the call of God to preach the gospel" as the Apostle Paul noted in scripture: "Christ did not send me to baptize, but to preach the gospel... *(1 Corinthians 1:17)*. For the sake of this book, **the call** was for the Pit Crew to join in prayer whenever church needs emerged.

Thoracic Cavity: the chamber of the body that houses the heart, lungs, rib cage walls, tendons and so on.

Time of Testing: referencing scripture that mentions "testing" in regards to trying or difficult times. See *Luke 8:13 (NIV* or *ESV).*

Tiniest: meaning tiny, smallest, the least or minuscule.

TMI: is an abbreviation for the phrase meaning: "too much information."

Toil: hard, continuous and exhausting labor.

Tongues (or Speaking in Tongues): is a highly debated topic among many Christians. But in this text, it refers to the verse *Mark 16:17* in KJV. There are 27 references to "tongues" in the KJV New Testament. *Tongues* is a reference to manifestation of the power and presence of God resting on the true believer. Because Pentecostal and charismatic beliefs are not uniform, there are many different theological views about speaking in tongues. But most agree it is a spiritual gift that is either human language or a supernatural heavenly language.

Trach: is an abbreviation for the word "tracheotomy;" an operation where patient's trachea is cut to allow air into the lungs.

Transfer of custody: when emergency personnel transport patients to hospital emergency rooms during medical crises, they must hand the patient over to the care of a doctor. They are not allowed to merely deliver someone without transferring their care to a qualified medical professional. Also see: *Direction of Care.*

Transform Tucson: a former ministry for prayer and service to Tucson's most needy population. As of the writing of this book, there was no evidence the group still exists. Could not verify contact information.

Treasure: accumulated true riches of great value and highly prized. Scripture refers to a treasure called the "Pearl of Great Price" *(Matthew 13:46).*

Trepidation: trembling, nervous or quivering fear, alarm, or agitation.

Upper Room: often said in reference to a room of prayer, *upper room* refers to the scripture where the Prayer Room of the disciples is revealed following Christ's crucifixion. The apostles met secretly in an "upper room" to pray and commiserate over the loss of their Savior Jesus. See *Acts 1:13-14.* In this book, GTTN has a prayer room located on the second floor above the sanctuary, which is called the Upper Room.

Utterance Gift: refers to speaking in tongues, a gift from the Holy Spirit to every believer who asks to be "filled with the Spirit of God." See "tongues" or "speaking in tongues in this glossary for a more thorough explanation.

Veracity: conformity to truthfulness; accuracy or factual.

Vestige: visible evidence of something no longer present.

Vito Andolini Corleone: (aka Don Corleone) is Mario Puzo's fictional character in the novel and 1972 movie of the same name, "The Godfather," who headed a fictitious mafia family.

Warrior: referring to an individual committed to pray. Warring in prayer is the mission of a prayer warrior experienced in warfare.

Wither: means to shrivel, fade, decay or dwindle away.

Word of the Lord: a common phrase among Christians referring to either the written Bible or a spoken word inspired by the Holy Spirit.

World of Darkness: The phrase is a colloquialism referencing demonic forces or potential devilish influences.

Zephyr: A gentle, mild breeze, or something fine or of light quality.

Bibliography

Butler, T. C., (1991). Holman Bible dictionary. *Holman Bible Publishers,* Nashville, Tennessee.

Dictionary.com, (2016). *Dictionary.com, LLC.* [Online dictionary, Website]. Retrieved from: http://www.dictionary.com/

ESV, (2001). *English Standard Version.* [Retrieved from: software]. Crossway Bibles, a ministry of the Good News Publishers, Wheaton, IL. Oxford University Press.

Francis Frangipane, (2015). Like A Watered Garden: Quotes/ Insights/ Revelations. *Arrow Publications. p. 10.* Cedar Rapids, Iowa.

GOD'S WORD, (1995). Copyright © 1995 by God's Word to the Nations Bible Society. All rights reserved. Retrieved from Bible software.

The Holy Bible, (1995). *God's Word.* Copyright © 1995 by God's Word to the Nations Bible Society. All rights reserved. [Retrieved from: software].

Holy Bible, *New International Version®.* (NIV®). Copyright © 1973, 1978, 1984, 2001 by Biblica, Inc.™ Used by permission. All rights reserved. [Retrieved from software].

Holy Bible, *New Living Translation®* (NLT), copyright © 1996, 2004 by Tyndale Charitable Trust. Used by permission of Tyndale House Publishers. All rights reserved.

Hooke, S. H., (1941). *Bible in Basic* English (BBE). [Retrieved from: software]. Cambridge England. Cambridge University Press.

KJV, (1611). *King James Bible*. [The KJV is public domain in the United States].

Medical Dictionary, (2016). The Free Dictionary. *Farlex*. [Online dictionary, Website]. *Retrieved from: http://medical-dictionary.thefreedictionary.com/coma.*

Merriam-Webster, (2015). Dictionary. Online dictionary. *Retrieved from: https://www.merriam-webster.com/*

NKJV, (1979). *New King James Bible*. Copyright 1979, 1980, 1982. *Published by HarperCollins*. [Retrieved from: software].

Peterson, E. H., (2002). *The Message*: *The Bible in Contemporary Language* © 2002 by Eugene H. Peterson. All rights reserved. [Retrieved from: software].

Randolph, L. J., (1998). *User Friendly Prophecy: Guidelines for the Effective Use of Prophecy*, Shippensburg, PA. Destiny Image, Publishers, Inc.,.

The Voice, (2014). *Hear the Voice*. Thomas Nelson. Thomas Nelson Inc. [Retrieved from: software].

Endnotes

i   *Matthew 11:15; Mark 4:9;* and *Luke 8:8,* "For those with ears to hear…"

ii   *Ephesians 2:4-10,* "But because of his great love for us, God, who is rich in mercy, made us alive with Christ even when we were dead in transgressions—it is by grace you have been saved. And God raised us up with Christ and seated us with him in the heavenly realms in Christ Jesus, in order that in the coming ages he might show the incomparable riches of his grace, expressed in his kindness to us in Christ Jesus. For it is by grace you have been saved, through faith—and this is not from yourselves, it is the gift of God—not by works, so that no one can boast. For we are God's handiwork, created in Christ Jesus to do good works, which God prepared in advance for us to do" *(NIV).*

iii *1 Corinthians 2:11,* "Who can see into a man's heart and know his thoughts? Only the spirit that dwells within the man. In the same way, the thoughts of God are known only by His Spirit" (The Voice). *1 Corinthians 2:14,* "But the natural man does not receive the things of the Spirit of God, for they are foolishness to him; nor can he know them, because they are spiritually discerned" *(NKJV).*

iv   *Ephesians 5:31-3,* "For this reason a man shall leave his father and mother and be joined to his wife, and the two shall become one flesh." This is a great mystery, but I speak concerning Christ and the church" *(NKJV).*

v   *Hebrews 13:8,* "Jesus Christ is the same yesterday, today, and forever *(NKJV).*

vi   Jesus said in *Luke 18:27,* "What is impossible with men is possible with God" *(ESV).*

vii *2 Corinthians 12:2-4,* "I know a man in Christ who fourteen years ago was caught up to the third heaven—whether in the body or out of the body I do not know, God knows. And I know that this man was caught up into paradise—whether in the body or out of the body I do not know, God knows—and he heard things that cannot be told, which man may not utter" *(ESV)*.

viii *Luke 12:7,* "But even the hairs of your head are numbered. Have no fear: you are of more value than a flock of sparrows" *(BBE)*.

ix *Matthew 15:18,* "But those things which proceed out of the mouth come from the heart...." *(NKJV)*.

x *Isaiah 61:10,* "I will greatly rejoice in the Lord, my soul shall be joyful in my God; For He has clothed me with the garments of salvation, He has covered me with the robe of righteousness, As a bridegroom decks himself with ornaments, and as a bride adorns herself with her jewels" *(NKJV)*.

xi *Philippians 3:21,* "Through His power to bring everything under His authority, he will change our humble bodies and make them like his glorified body" *(from GOD'S WORD Copyright © 1995 by God's Word to the Nations Bible Society. All rights reserved.)*.

xii *2 Corinthian 4:16,* "That is why we never give up. Though our bodies are dying, our spirits are being renewed every day" *(Holy Bible, New Living Translation ®, copyright © 1996, 2004 by Tyndale Charitable Trust. Used by permission of Tyndale House Publishers. All rights reserved)*.

xiii *Matthew 18:3,* Jesus said, "...Assuredly, I say to you, unless you are converted and become as little children, you will by no means enter the kingdom of heaven. Therefore whoever humbles himself as this little child is the greatest in the kingdom of heaven. Whoever receives one little child like this in My name receives Me" *(NKJV)*.

xiv *Exodus 33:20,* "......you cannot see My face, for no one may see Me and live" *(NIV)*.

xv *Matthew 28:20,* Jesus said, "...I am with you always, even to the end of the age. Amen" *(NKJV)*.

xvi *Job 33:4,* "The Spirit of God made me what I am, the breath of God Almighty gave me life!" *((from THE MESSAGE: The Bible in Contemporary Language © 2002 by Eugene H. Peterson. All rights reserved)*.

xvii *Matthew 1:23,* "...and they shall call His name Immanuel," which is translated, "God with us" *(NKJV)*.

xviii *Romans 8:2,* "And we know that all things work together for good to those who love God, to those who are the called according to His purpose" *(NKJV)*.

xix   *2 Timothy 4:22,* <u>The duties of a minister</u>: "...be instant in season, out of season."

xx   *Ephesians 6:18,* "praying always with all prayer and supplication in the Spirit, being watchful to this end with all perseverance and supplication for all the saints" *(NKJV).*

xxi   *Ezekiel 22:30,* "And I (God) sought for a man among them, that should make up the hedge, and stand in the gap before me for the land..." *(KJV).* And again scripture references intercession in *Isaiah 59:16,* *"He (God) saw that there was no man, and wondered that there was no intercessor" (NKJV).*

xxii   *John 11:4,* "This sickness is not unto death, but for the glory of God..." *(NKJV).*

xxiii   *Matthew 17:2,* "Jesus said to them, because of your little faith. For truly, I say to you, if you have faith like a grain of mustard seed, you will say to this mountain, 'Move from here to there,' and it will move, and nothing will be impossible for you" *(ESV).*

xxiv   *Acts 8:17,* "Then they laid hands on them, and they received the Holy Spirit" *(NKJV).*

xxv   *Deuteronomy 6:5,* "You shall love the Lord your God with all your heart, with all your soul, and with all your strength" *(NKJV).*

xxvi   *Acts 5:12",* "And by the hands of the apostles were many signs and wonders wrought among the people; (and they were all with one accord" *(KJV).*

xxvii   *2 Corinthians 3:18,* "But we all, with unveiled face, beholding as in a mirror the glory of the Lord, are being transformed into the same image from glory to glory, just as by the Spirit of the Lord *(NKJV).*

xxviii   *John 14:12,* "The person who trusts me will not only do what I'm doing but even greater things" *(The Message).*

xxix   *Numbers 14:22,* "Because all those men which have seen my glory, and my miracles, which I did in Egypt and in the wilderness" *(KJV).*

xxx   *John 14:6,* "Jesus said to him, "I am the way, the truth, and the life. No one comes to the Father except through Me" *(NKJV).*

xxxi   *Exodus 34:29,* "When Moses came down from Mount Sinai, with the two tablets of the testimony in his hand as he came down from the mountain, Moses did not know that the skin of his face shone because he had been talking with God" *(ESV).*

xxxii   *Psalms 139:23-24,* "Search me, O God, and know my heart: try me, and know my thoughts: And see if there be any wicked way in me, and lead me in the way everlasting" *(KJV).*

CPSIA information can be obtained
at www.ICGtesting.com
Printed in the USA
LVHW091738301220
675432LV00006B/309